CONFESSIONS OF A YOUNG PROPHET

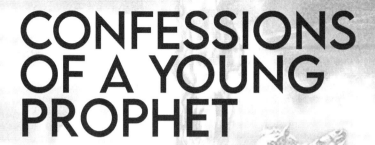

CONFESSIONS OF A YOUNG PROPHET

FOREWORD BY DR. MARK CHIRONNA

JUSTIN ALLEN

tall pine
BOOKS

"In John 1:14, the Bible declares that Jesus is the Word of God made flesh. Any time we sense God's presence, His Word is present. He imparts to us an awareness of who He is, and with His presence comes clarity concerning His will. Justin Allen, in his book, *Confessions of a Young Prophet*, gathers insights gleaned from his life as a gifted prophetic leader.

In these pages, Justin shares both the bumps and victories of hearing prophetically and learning to convey God's heart to others. The Word of God is the most powerful force in the universe. Our God spoke the entire Creation into being, and His Word now lives within each believer. Regardless of gifting or call, every believer has the privilege of learning to steward His Word/presence well."

—BILL JOHNSON
Bethel Church, Redding, CA
Author of *Open Heavens* and *Born for Significance*

"Justin Allen opens up his journal and invites you into a journey of discovery. The self-discovery is necessary to find your "voice" and recognize God's hand pulling you into destiny. With transparency and humor, he lets you see the vulnerable side of the prophetic call and gives you wisdom nuggets that will help you know Him better and allow the voice of the Lord to go out with impact and clarity!"

—JOHN E. THOMAS
President, *Streams Ministries, International*

"Justin Allen is a friend with a brilliant prophetic voice. In his latest writing, he challenges us with an out-of-the box perspective. He is also vulnerable and transparent in his words. This book will challenge your perspective and heart. Get ready for a fiery read!"

—RYAN LESTRANGE
Author of *Breaking Curses*

"Navigating the call of a prophet is not easy at any age or stage of life. Every prophet can point to seasons of crushing, hiddenness, exposure, suffering, and yes, ecstasy and glory. The call can come at any time and signals the start of an agonizing and vulnerable process to make ready the one called. There are some who try to shortcut the process, and some refuse it altogether, believing they can still fulfill the call powerfully and faithfully. It doesn't work. The process is a requirement.

It is lovingly administered by the hand of God to make one ready to be a mouthpiece for God. I've known Justin Allen for a long time now. He has submitted himself to the hand of God without reservation. *Confessions of a Young Prophet* is transparent, personal, and full of Scripture. The stories are not for entertainment, but they lay bare the sacredness and sobriety of the call to be a prophet. *Confessions of a Young Prophet* will help you understand and thrive in your own process of becoming a mouthpiece for God."

—DR. KIM M. MAAS
Kim Maas Ministries, Inc.
Author, *Prophetic Community & The Way of the Kingdom*

"A gift is not a merit badge that states you are better than another person. A gift is presented out of graciousness from a good, good Father. I love giving gifts. It is one of my favorite things to do as an earthly dad and granddaddy. When I do so, I feel like I am walking in one of the attributes of God the Father. Now there is another dimension to life as well. It goes something like this, "Spare the rod, and you will spoil the child."

But we don't talk too much about that nowadays. If we do, we might be labeled "child abusers" or some other unmentionable terms. But the sword of the Spirit is two-edged, and it cuts both ways. I know because I have been on the receiving end of our good, good Father, who is interested in character to carry the gift. Justin takes us on such a journey. Yes, we all fall down. But the nature of the authentic righteous ones is that we get back up, dust ourselves off, learn, and take another swing at this thing called life. I said life and not prophetic ministry. You must learn how to live a Christlike life and not just walk in a gift."

—JAMES W. GOLL
Founder of *God Encounters Ministries*
GOLL Ideation LLC

"This book that you hold in your hand by my friend Justin Allen is a well of wisdom. The weight of wisdom in this book to guide, instruct, encourage, and strengthen those called to the prophetic office is invaluable. It is not just a book you hold in your hands; it's a gift. It's a gift given to you from the heart of God through Justin.

The wisdom contained in these pages flowing from the heart of God will set you up for longevity, spiritual health, wholeness, and strength as you navigate the destiny upon your life. It is a plumbline, an incredible gift given to the prophetic movement from the Lord through Justin. Keep this book at a place of easy access because this is a well of wisdom to *continue* drinking from on your journey as one who is called to proclaim what is on the heart of the Lord, the prophetic voice of God."

—LANA VAWSER
Author of *The Prophetic Voice of God*, *A Time to Selah*,
and *I Hear the Lord Say "New Era"*

CONTENTS

FOREWORD

The term "prophetic" has become a buzzword of sorts in the current popular church culture. It clearly is used in both enthusiastic and scornful ways depending on who is talking about it. Much proliferation of "all things prophetic" lends itself to public scrutiny and examination, and rightly so. To claim one speaks on behalf of God is quite a bold claim. One that I would suggest needs to be done with knees knocking, heart palpitating, and voice shaking, honestly! Any sense of being cavalier about claiming to speak for God is so far from the testimony of Jesus that it cannot be considered a genuine expression of speech inspired by the work of the indwelling Spirit. In a day when so much abuse has taken place concerning the prophetic, there is a desperate need for reform, particularly within the larger independent Charismatic and Pentecostal movements.

The prophetic has to be approached with great humility and with the one who claims to offer inspired speech in particular situations, as having the character and the nature of Christ, namely walking in what Michael Gorman refers to as "cruciformity" and what Scot McKnight, to expand on Gorman's notion of the cross-shaped life, refers to as "Christoformity." The entire life of a disciple of Jesus is to be cross-shaped. Anything that falls short of what Matthias Wenk refers to as the "identity-forming narrative" of the Cross falls far short of genuine prophetic embodiment.

It is the psalmist who cries out, "Let the words of my mouth and the meditations of my heart be acceptable in Your sight, O Lord, my strength and my redeemer." So too, for prophetic expression to offer its highest good, the prophetic agent has to be utterly and totally dependent on the inwrought work of the Spirit to so constrain the heart in the love of Christ that the lips utter only that which is pleasing to God the Father on behalf of the Triune God, to those the agent is speaking to and making the claim that they are speaking on the Triune God's behalf.

Having established the criteria for genuine prophetic function in the Sermon on the Mount, Jesus speaks of the fact that living with Him as King of the Kingdom is costly, and prophets are no exception to the price that has to be paid. The ethical realities that must govern all speech somehow have to be integrated with the awareness of what occurred at Pentecost when the 120 began to speak with "other tongues." They began to speak "beyond themselves." Their words broke relational barriers that they carried and built bridges with those whose linguistic patterns and cultural preferences were not the same. At that moment when the mighty rushing wind of the Spirit filled the whole house where the 120 were sitting, and when the cloven tongues of fire sat on each of their heads, what was brought forth was what Roger Stronstad called, "the prophethood of all believers."

Stronstad is not implying that all believers are equal to those who carry the prophetic burden of those specifically called to that task in Ephesians 4. However, what Stronstad is saying is that the immersion into the fullness of the Spirit evokes from the Church as a whole a collective voice that bears witness to all people groups to the fact that Jesus is King and all nations will give allegiance to Him and thereby be freed from the limitations of sin, death, the grave, and hell itself.

There is a desperate need for a recovery of the testimony of Jesus, which indeed is the Spirit of Prophecy (Revelation 19:10) in this current hour. That testimony is cruciform, cross-shaped, and has to be embodied and not just talked about. God is looking for men and women who, not merely in their speech, but more importantly in their life, embody prophetic witness of the cross-shaped journey to glorification, as examples of what it means to be partakers of the divine nature. That being said, the Triune God is apprehending a generation of emerging young men and women whose allegiance to Christ is being tested for the purpose of giving them a voice. They are far from perfect, yet they are on a perfecting journey.

Justin Allen is one of those emerging voices. I have had the privilege of knowing Justin for the past decade or so, and I have come to appreciate the hand of God on his life and am aware of how God has invited him to grow in a grace that sometimes requires the kind of yieldedness to the cross that is costly. That yieldedness brings about the brokenness that lends itself to the release of the Spirit in his life, as Watchman Nee might say.

Justin invites you on a journey in this book into his own heart and life. He is endeavoring to be transparent and, like all of us, is a work in progress. There is much here to glean from for all of you on that road from brokenness to wholeness, where you are aware that brokenness and beauty coexist in you and shall until you receive your eternal reward. Take time to glean from Justin's transparency and allow the Spirit of Grace and Faith to take Justin's personal witness to Jesus and the Cross-Shaped Life (which is the Testimony of Jesus) to hear the Spirit of Prophecy in his words.

—Dr. Mark J Chironna, Bishop
Church On The Living Edge
Mark Chironna Ministries

INTRODUCTION

Justin Allen is a young prophet with a young family. He felt God led him to come to the Global School of Supernatural Ministry at the Global Awakening headquarters in Mechanicsburg, PA, where he completed the first and second years of school. I asked him to join two other young men to become my interns for his third year of training. He became one of the associate ministers of Global Awakening for a couple of years, after which he came to me and told me he felt like God was leading him to move to Tennessee with his family. Out of obedience to the Lord's call, he resigned his position as an associate of Global Awakening.

I have seen Justin weep before the Lord while experiencing God's heart for people and weep due to God's presence filling the room. I saw him read people's mail as he received prophetic words for them. He has a heart for evangelism. I had seen Justin in times when things were good in his life, experiencing the blessing of God and the favor of people. I also saw Justin in hard times when he wasn't experiencing the favor of people. Out of the crucible of pain, God has been teaching Justin more compassion and more humility. The important thing is that Justin remained faithful to God through the good times and the bad times, the joy and the pain.

You hold in your hands his first book, *Confessions of a Young Prophet*. I am introducing the author to you as one of his spiritual fathers. My prayer is for Justin to continue to be faithful to God and a learner during this season and to be one who is a father to others in the future.

—RANDY CLARK
DD, DMin, ThD, MDiv, BS, Religious Studies
Overseer of the *Apostolic Network of Global Awakening*
President of *Global Awakening Theological Seminary*

ONE
FRICTION, COMBUSTION, AND ASHES—WE ALL FALL DOWN

"When you speak, conviction will fall. People who aren't discerned will mistake this for criticism and resent you for it."

The words of a genuine prophet are heavy with both the goodness and glory of an omnipotent God, sharp and weighty in nearly every circumstance and situation. It is not always intentional or even welcomed by the mouthpiece, but it comes with the territory and office regardless of personal preference. The problem was it took me nearly twenty years of my life to realize my prophetic call and office.

Like a teenager navigating puberty, I was locked in a drastic transformation that literally altered me in every way and I was only along for the ride. Growing pains, significant mood swings, and strong inexpressible urges came from places appearing to develop overnight. I spent most of my time struggling to maintain my grip on social scenarios, relationships, and a general inability to understand people's lack of perspective.

I learned how to blend in externally, but at the expense of my spiritual and mental well-being. Managing my personal relationships and spiritual health simultaneously eluded me for years despite my best efforts and consistent pursuit of wholeness in that area of my life. I was learning valuable lessons about myself that I didn't value at the time. But I always had a strong awareness that I was *very* different from anyone who crossed my path. This awareness caused me to have questions as to why I was the way I was. During this period of time, I spent numerous untold seasons of my life wondering why I always seemed to be the component in nearly every scenario that caused either *friction* or *combustion*.

FRICTION

If I was to be in the midst of something, it was sure to accompany me, like an unwelcomed friend that never took a hint and disappeared. No matter how hard I tried, friction was like my shadow, a dark silhouette haunting my every move. It baffled me because I genuinely love people. I always enjoyed being in settings with lots of people—parties, social gatherings, malls, concerts, etc. While loving these situations, I found them draining and strangely exhausting. I thrived in one-on-one interaction but failed miserably at maintaining dialogue with groups of people. It felt shallow and a useless waste of time to me.

I prefered investing intensely in individual face-to-face interactions with depth and meaning rather than the frivolous pleasantries that felt empty and vain. Even now this is still my preference. But I place a more significant value on community than I did then because I now understand that different people receive differently due to the complex nature of the unique temperament of their personhood.

For as long as I can remember, I have always been intrigued with why people think and function the way they do. In these events, my love/hate relationship with social settings caused me to stumble into my place or comfort zone. I discovered it was far less exhausting to hide in the crowd, which allowed me to be around people without engaging with them. Balconies were awesome because I could observe the crowds in their natural state apart from the façade of how they wanted to be viewed. It was like a window into their soul for me. It was as if I could see thoughts forming before they manifested, like I had an unusual intuition.

A surprise was not a feeling with which I was well acquainted. It felt like I could predetermine the course of action with no factual information about the individual. It was subtle at first and very natural and familiar to such a degree I was virtually unaware of doing anything different than others would do. I noticed it when I pulled other people into my space; they would point out how different my process was from their journey. Essentially, I was *people watching*, but it was always more than that for me.

There was a deep pull inside me to *help* others by showing them adjustments they could make in their conduct, creating more opportunities than currently available before them, the third option, if you will. The problem was that this required interaction instead of simple observation. I was quickly made aware that almost no one was interested in what I thought they should do with their lives.

Apparently there was a reason all those social façades existed. These were barriers preventing access to those parts of themselves, obstacles that took time and energy to construct, and impediments they were not interested in moving. People fear what they don't understand and being misunderstood causes people to fear association with you. It was a long, consistent, and devastating realization for me to reach. Needless to say, this was the source of friction in nearly every consistent friendship I had. No one likes the one who exposes their flaws or brings light to their indiscretions. Without fail, prolonged friction leads to combustion.

COMBUSTION

Combustion is the act or process of burning—Oh, the burning.

In the early days it mainly consisted of burning bridges and destroying relationships, both good and bad, so I had no real handle on how to remain in them without causing them to self-destruct. I loved people deeply, but there was a problem. Whatever normal people have in their makeup that causes them to back off from an issue or overlook it in an attempt to save face or be civil didn't seem to be in me.

I had profound, passionate, and almost overwhelming conviction connected to viewpoints I would develop very quickly and could not seem to dismiss for the life of me. It was more than being opinionated; more like hardwired to operate in a fashion that was not conducive for keeping friendships. Like most, I was much more susceptible to my emotions in my teenage years and had a real problem with anger. I would come to understand that the external combustion that seemed to follow me everywhere I went was a byproduct of the internal combustion that was driving most of my endeavors.

I don't want to paint a picture as if I was some wayward teen causing trouble everywhere I went, leaving a trail of destruction in my wake. My parents raised me in a God-fearing home, and I can't remember not knowing about Jesus and had my conversion experience around the age of eight. From day one, they poured the Word into us and consistent prayer with lives lived in front of us aligned with what they taught us. They were prime examples of Christian parents and the ideal godly home, a greenhouse for spiritual growth, as well as a haven most will never know the privilege of experiencing.

My father was a deacon, Sunday school teacher, Jesus in the Easter play, and you name it, he did it. Mom was constantly preparing food for functions, families in need, or wherever was needed, and also teaching Sunday school, AWANA, nursery work, etc. Both of my parents sang regularly and were anointed to do so. Sunday mornings always consisted of the two of them practicing a new duet or Gospel song they were singing that day as Pillsbury cinnamon rolls baked in the oven. It is one of the many things they passed down that I'm extremely grateful for and have helped shape me into the man I am today.

A DAY OF RECKONING

I highlighted all of that to say this: Everyone goes through a process of discovering who they are, regardless of the home they're raised in or circumstances surrounding their childhood. Dr. Jay Strack, DMin, Luther Rice Seminary, uttered one of the most profound statements that thrust me into a deeper relationship with Jesus at the Kingdom youth conference in the year 2000, "There comes a time when the boys and girls have to sit down, and the men and women have to stand up."

There comes a day of reckoning, a moment when you realize your life is about much more than yourself. So you make a conscious choice to be proactive in pursuing your destiny, purpose, or a more excellent plan for your life. There will be multiple moments of marking along the way, but a handful stands above the rest. You will quickly discover a realm of warfare that seemingly manifests overnight—so, congratulations because you answered the call! The only question that remains is whether or not you'll continue to answer that call from here on out. Your parents can't make that choice, and your pastor won't do it for you—that responsibility rests on your shoulders.

Will you embrace the cross set before you that opens the doors of your destiny?

For me, initially answering the call had nothing to do with the prophetic and everything to do with the *cross* and what a slow death it was. I didn't grow up in an environment familiar or receptive to the spiritual gifts that now became the bedrock of my walk with Jesus, which all we knew then was the Southern Baptist realm. Honestly, to this day I'm incredibly grateful for the experience and high regard for Scripture instilled in me from a young age.

I'd always had this deep love for the church, worship, and the general experience of the saints coming together in one accord. It felt like everything made the most sense to me; it felt like home and still does. In our stream, the general progression and sign of maturity and growth primarily centered around knowledge of the Word, with a heavy emphasis on Bible college, seminary, and those little letters that come before your name. It was the natural progression in my pursuit of the Lord, and I dove into it. I took to the Bible like a duck to water and decided to invest everything I had in the Word. It made perfect sense to me that if I could know Him well, I would know everything I needed to know.

Now is the time to remind you that this is a collection of stories, experiences, and lessons learned throughout the course of my life thus far, and in no way is it chronological. My apologies for the way my mind works, but this is what you get with me. An honest look at the lives of believers, well known and unknown, requires a genuine examination of failure, disappointment, and the frustrations that drive us forward into our breakthroughs and successes.

Despite my best efforts and genuine pursuit of the Lord, I stumble, fall, and repeat this process regularly . But like I said before, answering the call is a perpetual process. It's not enough that you said yes last week, but there has to be a consistent resounding *yes* in your spirit that drives you and pushes you past the temptation of complacency.

I received one of those strong marking experiences on a mission trip to Honduras, where I accepted the call to a life of ministry, whatever that is. In all seriousness, it was a genuine shift in my life that altered everything forever. My perception of being called and ministry was minimal then, but it was enough to do what needed to be done. There was a boldness deposited in me then that would do nothing but grow from that moment forward.

The shy, quiet boy who would never speak in a group larger than three people was long gone, never to be seen again. He was replaced with a fiery, authoritative tone and a strong desire to lead in every scenario he entered. Many years later, I received my prayer language in a subsequent baptism, but a distinct burning in my spirit initiated that day and has yet to dwindle. I got what the prophet Jeremiah spoke of, *But His word was in my heart like a burning fire Shut up in my bones. I was weary of holding it back, And I could not* (Jeremiah 20:9, NKJV). This fire would prove to be, for lack of better words, a blessing and a curse.

ASHES AND WE ALL FALL DOWN

The thing about a fire burning inside of you is that it will remove wood, hay, and stubble in your life consistently until only precious metals remain. It's a slow burn, thorough and resolute. You can rest assured it will see the job through.

> For no other foundation can anyone lay than that which is laid, which is Jesus Christ. Now if anyone builds on this foundation with gold, silver, precious stones, wood, hay, straw, each one's work will become clear; for the Day will declare it, because it will be revealed by fire; and the fire will test each one's work, of what sort it is. If anyone's work which he has built on it endures, he will receive a reward. If anyone's work is burned, he will suffer loss; but he himself will be saved, yet so as through fire. Do you not know that you are the temple of God and that the Spirit of God dwells in you? If anyone defiles the temple of God, God will destroy him. For the temple of God is holy, which temple you are (1 Corinthians 3:11-17, NKJV).

Smith Wigglesworth, often referred to as the Apostle of Faith and a pioneer of the Pentecostal revival, made this penetrating statement, "God had broken me a thousand times before He brought me to this point."

So is the case with every great man and woman of God. Brokenness is a prerequisite to be used mightily by the Lord. The methods vary, but the desired results are the same. Obedience, humility, and compassion aren't attributes you're capable of imparting until integrated into your personhood. It brings me to one of the most beautiful things about the nature of our God and King—restoration.

His ability to make all things new is not limited by time, space, percentages, or popular opinion. The heart of the Trinity is reconciliation, and the pulse of the words ebb and flow with a piercing yet resounding truth throughout the ages and forevermore. We all fall down, we all fail miserably, but He's able and more than willing to make beauty from ashes. *To console those who mourn in Zion, to give them beauty for ashes, The oil of joy for mourning, The garment of praise for the spirit of heaviness* (Isaiah 61:3, NKJV).

CAREFULLY HANDLING THE PROPHETIC WORD

The very heart of the prophetic will always be the heart of the Father who did not send His Son into the world to condemn the world, but that the world through Him may be saved. A Father who was in the Son reconciling the world to Himself! There is no more incredible privilege than partnering with the Trinity, calling beauty out of the ash piles and seeing joy birthed out of the midst of adversity through the spoken word initiating the glorious response of praise!

There is glory on the words of a prophet that is distinctly different than other offices. Not greater, not better, but unique unto itself and must be appreciated and grasped lest it be cast to the wayside in an inability to receive the distinct razor-sharp ministry that is the Word of the Lord. While many prophetic ministers err by being harsh, insensitive, and emotionally distant, this does not mean the ministry does not carry a sting and a sharp edge in which to cut off what must be eradicated for your best interest. Viewing it as a sword, we must understand how to use it with excellence and precision so as not to harm those we attempt to help. It is vital that we do not slice them down while trying to cut entanglements off of them that would easily hinder them from the path of their destiny.

In early wartime surgery, they would often amputate limbs that could have easily been saved if they would have only taken the time to assess the situation appropriately. If a person's spiritual mobility is hindered rather than improved by our prophetic involvement in their lives, we must reevaluate our methods. It is never about how awesome we look with the sword in our hands, but rather how well we have protected, defended, and assisted the body of Christ in their pursuit of the King! We must lay our lives down for the sake of the bride; anything less is a disservice to the blood and body of Jesus.

Perpetually abiding in the Father is the only way to operate successfully in the spirit of prophecy, which is the testimony of Jesus, reflecting Christ in all we do and speak. While there are lessons to be learned via prophetic fathering and mothering, it will never replace the responsibility of individual communion with Abba God. You will never grasp the tone, timing, and precision that come with immediately responding to the whisper of the One who spoke it all into existence. Acts 17:28 tells us that it is in Him that we live and move and have our being. Paul uses a didactic poem where the verbs are used with a precise philosophical significance. No words can better express our constant dependence on God.

There is so much truth wrapped up in such a small piece of Scripture, which is the only way to live according to divinely created value and identity. Life, movement, and our very existence flow from the throne of grace where Jesus is seated on the mercy seat at the Father's right hand, interceding on our behalf! Why would we ever attempt to flow from any other place? It is vanity to attempt to operate successfully in the supernatural apart from anything less than total and complete surrender to decrees from the throne room.

THE TRINITY, A COMMUNITY OF THREE

Some may have difficulty jumping from illustrations about closeness and accessibility to God the Father and intimacy with Jesus while referencing the Holy Spirit. I even hear the Lord highlighting the concerns and questions being raised in the reader's mind like, *Which one is it? Father, Son, or Holy Spirit?* To that I respond, "Yes!" Believers must stop our efforts to separate the Godhead. We have made distinctions, rules, and protocols regarding the Trinity that is not in our best interest or the interests of those on the outside looking in.

The Trinity is not something placed before us in which we get to choose who we like the most; it is all or nothing. We get imbalanced, partial, and damaging prophetic perspective when we make this approach. Prophecy should always tip the scales back into *balance*, which is *justice* from a biblical perspective.

As Charles Spurgeon stood to preach his first sermon as pastor of New Park Street Chapel, he held his Bible in his hand and the doctrine of God in his heart. Then the young preacher exclaimed, "Nothing will so enlarge the intellect, nothing so magnifies the whole soul of man, as a devout, earnest, continued investigation of the great subject of the Deity." The Trinity in Unity and Unity in Trinity was not an optional appendage to the Gospel, rather a "gospel without belief in the living, and true God... [was] a rope of sand." Spurgeon believed that the Trinity was the key to theology.

One God, with complex and intricate characteristics—you cannot know Him entirely apart from constant contact and connection. If you have an issue with one, you have an issue with all. They are inseparable and fully interconnected at all times in all seasons. The unique expression does not denote separation but rather a greater heavenly reality in which seemingly opposite characteristics enhance the whole and flow effortlessly in one unified purpose.

The relational reality of the Father, Son, and Holy Spirit must be a pillar in your life if you intend to operate in a prophetic ministry that bears any fruit. While there may be moments you feel one of the three is taking the lead in the flavor of the expression, it is essential that your prophetic declaration be directed by a healthy relational paradigm of the three working in unity to accomplish a central goal. There will be an unadulterated and pure flow of prophetic power when you have a mature view of all three.

I once heard Dr. Mark Chironna say, "People don't see the world around them the way it is; they see the world around them the way they are!" I propose that this statement is true and weighty in regard to prophetic ministry. The idea that you can minister prophetically through a distorted lens and relational view of the Godhead should be a sobering and scary thought.

Prophesying from a place of personal frustration, irritation, or disappointment doesn't make you a false prophet; it just makes you a bad prophet. Personal stewardship is paramount in the life of those who operate in a gift given absent from repentance. I will unpack this idea later on in the book. Still, I wanted to introduce the thought for you to chew on as we move forward in this compilation of experiences intended to call you higher in the area of intimacy in the prophetic.

Take this time to ask the Father, Son, and Holy Spirit to search the innermost parts of your mind, will, and emotions and let the refining fire of God be put to every area. As we go chapter by chapter, I believe you will be reminded of past hurt, triggered, convicted, moved to repentance, and strangely encouraged as the Holy Spirit highlights what must be removed in your life so that more of His presence may be a reality.

I believe there is power in the testimony and releasing the anointing from my life to yours as you "receive a prophet in the name of a prophet." I invite you to enter into a revelatory experience with the very spirit of prophecy as you read, reflect, and repair the breaches in the walls of your heart throughout this book. I declare that you will prophesy, you will declare the Word of the Lord, stewarding your gifts with excellence for the glory of God!

2

REQUIREMENTS FOR REVELATION

"AN INVITATION TO AUTHORITY"

R*evelation is an invitation to abide in a greater reality.* It is an invitation to come up higher in the Spirit while going deeper into the secret places and facets of His unfailing love for us. In its simplest form, it beckons us to drink deeply from a fountain whose source is heaven and whose end has yet to be reached.

> *"Eye has not seen, nor ear heard, Nor have entered into the heart of man The things which God has prepared for those who love Him. But God has revealed them to us through His Spirit. For the Spirit searches all things, yes, the deep things of God" (1 Corinthians 2:9, 10, NKJV).*

In a culture enamored with the next big thing, getting your mail read, radical manifestations, and supernatural experiences, one must not forget the Source from which all blessings flow. As an advocate for divine encounters, I believe in the supernatural power of the Holy Spirit. But we must not become so consumed with the encounter that we neglect communion with the God of the encounter. If forced to choose between revelation or an encounter, I will choose revelation every time. It is due to the reality that all revelation flows from encounters, but all encounters do not necessarily contain a revelation. To say they are equal would be incorrect, but they are connected, nonetheless. Becoming a people of His presence is vital and not merely a distant witness to His involvement in the lives of others. *Revelation flows*, meaning one must be connected to remain in a lifestyle of consistent communication with the hosts of heaven that the purposes of that Kingdom might be established here in this earthly realm.

THE SEARCH IS REQUIRED

While revelation is not a thing to be earned, it is also not a thing liberally distributed to those who haphazardly walk through life disconnected and directionless. *It is the glory of God to conceal a matter, but the glory of kings is to search out a matter* (Proverbs 25:2, NKJV).

Seek and find—there must be some level of pursuit, hunger, and a desire to go after Him with all your heart. He conceals things because He loves us. He enjoys the relationship and character that is built on having to search it out. The entire idea of revelation is the act of unveiling something previously veiled.

The goal is not solely in what is hidden now being accessible, but the glory is in the process of uncovering and the beauty that is released. Like a child opening gifts on Christmas, the joy they experience as they tear the paper away revealing what was previously unknown! *The secret things belong to the LORD our God, but the things revealed belong to us* (Deuteronomy 29:29, NKJV). When we lose our sense of wonder, then adventure and pursuit quickly evaporate. In failing to pursue, we fail to apprehend, and when we fail to apprehend, we will never have the opportunity to steward the gift.

The grace gifts are by no means earned, but they can most definitely mature into a place of greater discernment and accuracy as we move from glory to glory.

For the gifts and the calling of God are irrevocable (Romans 11:29, NKJV).

If you did nothing to get them, then you can do nothing to lose them. If you use your free will to ignore the nudging of those giftings, over time your heart will become callous, causing the inner witness of the Holy Spirit to dim faintly. It is not indicative of removing the ability but rather an absence of the medium through which the gift moves fluidly. Often people mistakenly assume the capacity is no longer there when in reality they neglected the process empowering them to operate in the fullness of Who created them to be.

THE DARK SIDE OF POWER

Though the gifts can be manipulated through the demonic, witchcraft, sorcery, and other evil sources, they will never function at full capacity apart from the real source of power, the Spirit of the living God.

Psychics have the capacity to move in surprising levels of accuracy absent from the ministry of the Holy Spirit. Witches and warlocks can function in supernatural power apart from the movement of the Holy Spirit in their respective scenarios. They do not lose their ability to perform, even at high levels, while living amid the darkness. Let me clearly state that I do not think any of the above are *valid* expressions of spiritual gifting. I believe they are distortions of *prophetic* and *seer* giftings significantly manipulated by their environment and a general lack of light.

I also believe many in the occult are much more knowledgeable in the supernatural area than the average Christian. The primary difference is the spirit in which they operate. Real power comes from the Creator who defines the gifts and holds the keys to our fullest potential.

While there is a measure of *power* to be attained through demonic powers, principalities, and practices, the fallout is devastating in the lives of those involved. There is a profound long-term consequence in abandoning the Father of lights to pursue the father of lies.

WHY CHOOSE THE DARK SIDE?

There are various reasons people choose to exchange the Giver of the gifts for the manifestation of the gifting. The reasons range from ignorance to the extreme of willful disobedience. In my experience, people seldom segregate themselves by their own choice, and life has a way of taking its toll on those living the consequences. History shows us the world is less than kind to those going against the grain and challenging the status quo. People tend to grow very comfortable amid complacency in a society that sets the bar low for the general populous while leaving it quite high for a select few in leadership. Unique expression comes with a high cost in a society needing reformation. Remember, who we celebrate today as historical reformers were frequently the thorn in the side of the culture, but they were destined to have the ultimate impact.

I spent the last few paragraphs addressing the opposite side of the supernatural regarding giftings. It is imperative not to ascribe value to your ministry or the ministry of anyone else based solely on the expression of gifting or ability in their life. Gifting and godly leadership are two very different things. One is an unconditional gift absent from repentance, and the other indicates great character and submission to God and His purposes towards the hearts of men and women. However, gifting under the submission of the Holy Spirit inside the realm of godly leadership creates a supernatural breakthrough in every area it touches. God's heart for His Church is that our gifts be on display in all their splendor while under the leading of the Spirit of God.

My concern is that the current expression of the Church , in many ways, is responsible for the great falling away into the occult by those who were once part of our congregations and communities. By no means will I make a blanket statement or negate the personal responsibility of those living in iniquity, but I reserve this mention.

The negligence, ignorance, and poor teaching concerning the gifts and their expression in times past was in so many ways the stumbling block that caused many to fall into the pit where they are currently entrenched. Fear of the unknown and hesitancy to incorporate the diversity of gifting into the local church in so many ways signed the death warrant on those who did not fit their mold. Many flocked into the church seeking love, acceptance, and a place to serve utilizing their God-given gifts. Sadly, they were met with a suppressing fear that either capped their expression or kicked them to the curb.

I believe some of the most significant apostles, prophets, pastors, teachers, and evangelists are currently trapped in the occult. Why? Simply because they first came to the church but found no place there for them to express their God-given gift. We must repent and then pursue those in bondage by raising a standard in our own lives that make no place for intimidation or fear regarding the gifting of our brothers and sisters. Purpose in your heart to define those around you by what the Father says about them and not giving place to the devil in your perception of those around you.

> *"Ask, and it will be given to you; seek, and you will find; knock, and it will be opened to you. For everyone who asks receives, and he who seeks finds, and to him who knocks it will be opened" (Matthew 7:7-8, NKJV).*

ABUSE OF POWER

Stewardship is the doorway to increase and its pathway to dominion. Kings have dominion, authority, and influence on a greater level than the average citizen. Adding to this kingship, the ministry of the priesthood, you have a Melchizideckian ministry, which is the ministry of Christ in its most basic form. I believe the prophet, priest, and king model is a more accurate representation of the new covenant prophetic ministry. There is a common misconception among charismatic Christians, particularly in the area of intercession and prayer, that *authority* is somehow "taken"... Phrases like, "I take authority over this _____ (add spirit of _____ for good measure), in the name of Jesus!" It sounds impressive and may feel right, but it is the farthest thing from the truth.

Authority is not apprehended; authority is exercised! You will fail miserably if you attempt to minister in a place of authority instead of from a place seated in heavenly places with Christ Jesus. You cannot fake authority because with it comes power. Related to the Holy Spirit, this power is a catalyst towards freedom and liberty. The counterfeit authority coming from the devil carries an oppressive control level that enslaves them by its connection. There is virtually no comparison between the two types of authority!

The problem lies with the majority of religious institutions rooted in a stronghold of control ascertained by religious tactics teaching us to work for acceptance, authority, and freedom instead of from it. In most of my interactions with believers raised in organized religious or denominational settings, the concept of the biblical authority I'm referring to would be foreign.

Strongholds are predominantly tied to patterns of thought, and these patterns flow from past experience and the emotions tied to those events. When this occurs, emotional responses are formed on multiple levels of our being, particularly the deepest places of our soul. If unaware of this, we will continue to operate in a gift absent from repentance flowing through a dirty conduit.

BEING ACCOUNTABLE IN A RECKLESS WORLD

The stream of revelation coming from heaven is perfectly pure but must first flow through you before it gets to them. The issue is never the source, how it gets from the source to the recipient. Unresolved issues in your soul can steal glory from the King of Kings and Lord of Lords. Understanding this should create a sense of godly fear and reverence to rest on all who call themselves messengers of God.

Make no mistake; grace does not eliminate removing accountability in your life. To be accountable requires giving an account of your ability. A world where anyone can say anything and no one is responsible for the words they speak in the name of the Lord degenerates into chaos and disorder and mocks the spirit of prophecy, which is the testimony of Jesus.

The challenges associated with being a prophetic person are numerous but not problematic. The opposition you experience and the consistent learning curve connected to a life filled with ecstatic encounters, the deep knowings, and fiery mandates from heaven are enough to bring you to your knees in a sobering awareness that apart from God, you can do nothing. It is human nature to resist pain, discomfort, and unfamiliar territory. But the prophets do not get this luxury because they are often forged in the fire of adversity until every wayward motive in their heart is smashed into pieces. As Uncle Ben in *Spider-Man* said, "With great power comes great responsibility."

While gifts are absent from repentance, your character, integrity, and condition of your heart matter greatly to the Lord. The ministry of the prophet conveys the words of God and the Father's heart to the world around them. To think that God is not concerned with an accurate representation of Himself is a radical error. The prophet's high calling comes with great opportunity for glory but the potential for catastrophe should we treat it as common and unholy.

> *If anyone speaks, let him speak as the oracles of God. If anyone ministers, let him do it as with the ability which God supplies, that in all things God may be glorified through Jesus Christ, to whom belong the glory and the dominion forever and ever (I Peter 4:11, NKJV).*

I pray that as you pursue the heart of the Father through prophetic revelation, you accept the invitation in deeper levels of wholeness, higher expressions of the character of Christ, and a more balanced perspective of the heart of God towards humanity. May the presence and power of God reconstruct you from the ground up in your knowledge of Him. I declare clarity over your mind, rest over your physical body, and shalom over your emotions. I pray the deep places in God minister to the deep places in you as you submit to the sovereign hand of the Lord, molding you into His image from grace to grace.

Deep calls unto deep at the noise of Your waterfalls (Psalm 42:7, NKJV).

3

ACCUSATION, SLANDER, BETRAYAL

"The devil will always attack your character, family, and reputation. Not necessarily in that order."

The devil is a liar—but this does not mean he lacks the capacity to tell the truth. The reality is quite contrary; he loves to manipulate the truth by painting an alternate picture of reality for you to view. He will consistently, strategically, and systematically attempt to dismantle you in these three areas. Though not of the opinion that all difficulties we experience in life are related to spiritual warfare, I recognize from experience that these areas are specific areas of emphasis for warfare in my life.

My thoughts and musings on the topic are attempts to equip those who read this to bypass long-term roadblocks to their destiny by making them aware of any opposition coming their way. The most challenging battles fought are the ones you fail to realize you are in the midst of now.

As you read this, ask the Holy Spirit to make you aware of the areas you are most susceptible to stumbling through your personal development. Taking an honest evaluation of yourself will allow you to safeguard your heart against brokenness and long-term relational wounds the enemy would love to inflict upon you. Being mindful of this will improve your ability to assess your longstanding progress accurately.

And He said to me, "My grace is sufficient for you, for My strength is made perfect in weakness." Therefore most gladly I will rather boast in my infirmities, that the power of Christ may rest upon me. Therefore I take pleasure in infirmities, in reproaches, in needs, in persecutions, in distresses, for Christ's sake. For when I am weak, then I am strong (2 Corinthians 12:9-11, NKJV).

CHARACTER

Character is who you are and what you do when no one is watching. The reason Satan attacks so many in this area is simple; many believers leave this arena unprotected. A prophet cannot afford to leave any area of their life unprotected for the enemy to wreak havoc. For some their issue is lying, others it's money, and for many, it's sexual sin. Regardless of your area of weakness, Christ is sufficient to transform weakness into a beautiful display of glory, pointing to the power of Jesus at work inside of you.

The issue of character is not perfection but a commitment to seeing the reality of the power of the cross manifested in your life. Greater is He who is in you than he who is in the world. One of the reasons I spend so much of my time and resources teaching young prophetic people and leaders of all areas of influence is to teach the distinction between their gifting and character. Your gifting comes without repentance or even to have it revoked. *For the gifts and the calling of God are irrevocable* (Romans 11:29, NKJV).

Your gifting and anointing will create a way into the places you're supposed to be (*and some places you aren't supposed to be*). Every open door is not one you are supposed to go through. However, your character will keep you in places where your gifting and ability cannot.

Character is the foundation on which your gifting and anointing are sustained. The flawed character will result in an unstable foundation that will radically limit your ability to go to higher places in the Spirit. Attacks on character are generally subtle yet consistent, hitting you in an area of perceived weakness until you begin to submit to the pressure of reaction rather than the actions led by the Spirit of God.

By default, one of the very things that builds character is your ability to stand firm without wavering when called into question. The idea is that you can stand on your own when under the scrutiny of those around you. It is essential because you have the provisions necessary to protect yourself from those with malicious intent that seek to destroy you in the court of popular opinion. Because whether or not you have faced this already, rest assured, it is coming in one form or another.

Therefore, having been justified by faith, we have peace with God through our Lord Jesus Christ, through whom also we have access by faith into this grace in which we stand and rejoice in hope of the glory of God. And not only that but we also glory in tribulations, knowing that tribulation produces perseverance; and perseverance, character; and character, hope. Now hope does not disappoint because the love of God has been poured out in our hearts by the Holy Spirit who was given to us (Romans 5:1-5, NKJV).

The manifestation of our justification often comes on the backside of tribulation. But peace is reachable through sustaining grace that keeps us amidst great tribulation. Character exists in the seed form of the core values, thought patterns, and ideals you embrace in your mind. Frequently those seeds must be buried in the mud of accusation and slander before they take root, break through, and bear tangible fruit in your life. Your convictions are immaterial until they are put to the test in real life.

Some may find this portion of the book quite abrasive with little regard for emotional disposition or tone. If that appears to be the case, then so be it. The objective in this chapter is not intended to cater to emotion or empathetic disposition. I do not want to minister to your feelings. I aim to challenge them along with any other vain ambitions or illusions of grandeur. The purpose and role of a prophet are not for personal edification but the glorification and manifestation of the person of Jesus Christ.

God, who at various times and in various ways spoke in time past to the fathers by the prophets, has in these last days spoken to us by His Son, whom He has appointed heir of all things, through whom also He made the worlds; who being the brightness of His glory and the express image of His person, and upholding all things by the word of His power, when He had by Himself purged our sins, sat down at the right hand of the Majesty on high, having become so much better than the angels, as He has by inheritance obtained a more excellent name than they (Hebrews 1:1-4, NKJV).

The nature of the role of the prophet is that their lives are often indistinguishable from the message they carry. Prophets are a tangible manifestation of the word of the Lord to the world around them. Because of this, there is a high call to personal consecration and a life laid down at a higher level than the average believer. The moment you decide to embrace the glory that comes with death is when you move toward a lifestyle of resurrection power.

Therefore, brethren, we are debtors—not to the flesh, to live according to the flesh. For if you live according to the flesh you will die; but if by the Spirit you put to death the deeds of the body, you will live. For as many as are led by the Spirit of God, these are sons of God. For you did not receive the spirit of bondage again to fear, but you received the Spirit of adoption by whom we cry out, "Abba, Father." The Spirit Himself bears witness with our spirit that we are children of God, and if children, then heirs—heirs of God and joint heirs with Christ, if indeed we suffer with Him, that we may also be glorified together (Romans 8:12-17).

The Spirit's leading is nonnegotiable in the Kingdom, especially for those cloaked in the mantle of a prophet. We often forget that the Holy Spirit led Jesus into the wilderness to be tested by the devil (Matthew 4:1). We neglect to meditate on the reality that Jesus learned obedience through the things He suffered (Hebrews 5:8). God is not opposed to increasing the fire on your life to produce purity, consecration, and a greater manifestation of sanctification than you have previously walked in.

It is imperative to recognize these moments and embrace the fire, allowing us to be cleansed of the impurities that might ultimately disqualify us from the Kingdom work for which we are destined. God is good, but His ways often elude us when we choose activity over intimacy. Changing how we think will result in our hearts and the methods we aim to draw near to God. Concerning intimacy with God, we must tune our ear to the whispers of God so we may move into deeper things.

Character is an inside job. God can only help you with what you give Him access to. So take a moment, do an inventory of the thoughts and intents of your heart, and provide unconditional access to the Father of lights that He might illuminate the dark spaces. In doing so, you will fortify yourself against the tricks of the enemy through simple, pure, life-giving intimacy.

FAMILY

Few areas have been attacked with greater intentionality and consistency than that of the family unit. I believe the devil knows there is no more critical source of stability, accountability, and comfort than the family unit.

The duality of Father and husband are two of the primary ways God reveals Himself. As Jesus is the eternal Son of God, so the body of Christ is the bride. The relational dynamics expressed are more than stories or nostalgic little philosophies but are a literal invitation into a Kingdom superseding this realm and all others.

It is a covenant worth fighting for, and the devil knows it. This is why he works overtime in the lives of every believer to destroy relationships and communication keeping us isolated in a place of powerlessness.

The Bible states that if anyone wants to enter the Kingdom, they must become like a child, potentially confusing or even exclusive if you overthink it. But I believe it's an invitation to live on a higher plane, not limited by the sting of impossibilities, disappointment, or the heartaches failure brings. Frequently we carry distorted views of reality inherited from our families. Baptism into the family of God allows us to drop that baggage at the door, whose name is Jesus, and we enter into a new reality absent from worst-case scenarios.

Maybe your family line contains broken relational

paradigms due to the pain of significant loss, addiction, violence, infidelity, or any number of horrible examples. The Bible tells us that if any man (or woman) be in Christ, they are a new creature, and the old is past, and behold, He is making all things new. The idea is this: for a child, everything they are experiencing is new.

There is no grid for hopelessness, heartache, or propensity to get stuck in ruts of depression. If we can identify the most outstanding areas of disappointment, we can, in short order, reframe those scenarios in a way that makes room for glory. It is a framework causing all things to work together for those who love God and are called according to His purposes. Where previously we saw only opposition, now we have the opportunity to overcome by the blood of the Lamb and the word of our testimony. The testimony of a son or daughter is deeply loved by a good Father that constantly works all things for our good.

The family paradigm is foundational for success, where we find purpose, comfort, companionship, and accountability. How we have experienced family does not, in any way, mirror heaven's definition. In healthy families, love trumps agreement, and covenant overrides name and rank. Love covers a multitude of sins, and the context of the family provides unlimited opportunities to cover the indiscretions, shortcomings in the most vulnerable of contexts.

Within the prophetic teaching and culture, a subtle ideology crept in and somehow exalted the prophetic gift, office, and operation above the context of service and submission. While there are probably many places this has surfaced, it is time we bury it, along with the pride and arrogance that brought it up in the first place. An unhealthy, independent spirit arises, which is actually a demonic imitation of the identity movement, aiming to elevate the individual while glorifying themselves at the expense of those around them. It is self-seeking, demonic at the core, exalting soulish ambitions through exercising the gifts but absent from fruit of the Spirit. Rest assured, the moment you step away from godly counsel, accountability, and the context of a biblical definition of family, a dilemma suddenly appears. God initiated the family unit and has every intention of sustaining it. The sooner you embrace this, the quicker you will see genuine, lasting success in every area of your life.

Family is far more challenging in reality than theory, mainly because it involves free will and people with radically different viewpoints, convictions, and core values. Most partnerships formed in this world are mutually beneficial and based on shared values with a common goal. The family is not a goal-oriented organism; it is a dynamic, challenging medium that requires sacrifice to function.

Compromise is a word that gets a bad rap, especially in most charismatic Christian circles. It is often used to imply a failure of some sort. Within the context of a healthy relationship, there must be a consistent compromise for mutual submission to occur.

The biblical definition of love is simple: sacrifice. This is how we know what love is: Jesus Christ laid down

his life for us. And we ought to lay down our lives for
our brothers and sisters (1 John 3:16, NIV).

If you don't sacrifice, then you don't love. Jesus
demonstrated this on the cross at the instruction of the
Father. Often this is put to the test in seemingly minus-
cule acts of service. There is something holy about considering others above yourself that develops a stronghold of love, destroying a self-seeking, self-serving way
of thinking that robs you of deep and meaningful expressions of love. Apart from real love, any success you experience will be fleeting and lacking the weight your life
was destined to carry.

One primary element of the family dynamic is the
covenant of marriage. In many years of ministry I had
the opportunity to witness firsthand the radical devasta-
tion caused by sin, compromise, and selfishness. Divorce
is a reality for many due to circumstances outside of their
control.

Unholy, unhealthy teaching on the subject has
caused many to move from years of abuse to a life of condemnation simply because they chose to move forward
rather than living in fruitless relationships marked by
abuse and brokenness. I would say there is nothing sa-
cred or holy about sacrificing the call of God on your life
due to the continued, willful disobedience of another.
The stigma surrounding this subject and the continued,
unnecessary suffering it causes in the lives of so many believers is drive enough to address this. If divorce has been
your reality, I encourage you to learn from the pain, find

a place where you can grow, and use it as a launchpad to go where you are called to go.

These words will sting and are painful to process and extremely difficult to embrace for some. You must understand that this is okay. I do not write these words to condemn or shame you, but I write these words for you to experience freedom. Or at least it sets you on course towards a place where that can become a reality in your life.

Life happens, and you cannot control others or the outcomes of their decisions. You can, however, purpose in your heart to respond in a way that is holy and above reproach. While this may manifest in a multiplicity of ways, you alone will stand before God and answer for the condition of your heart in the wake of heartache and disappointment.

For those who fought with all your heart, soul, mind, and strength only to find yourself defeated, take heart, for the promises of God are not out of reach. The Father has a way of turning brokenness into breakthroughs and using broken hearts as a catalyst for a fresh start. So regardless of where you find yourself in this current hour, God's heart for you is that you find comfort, solace, and restoration in a family that reflects heaven.

REPUTATION

At this point you may be thinking, *Where are the confessions?* But first I want to give you some practical foundational principles through teaching that you see enacted in a real-life scenario. If any one of these areas is lacking or underdeveloped, your battle may fail to end in a redemptive fashion. Character is nonnegotiable, family is a necessity, and reputation, at some point, will be thrown on that altar of your life to see if you value vanity above the purity of heart. The question remains, what will you do when faced with this reality?

Many loved Jesus, but many also hated Him. The Son of Man was known as a friend of sinners, accused of being a whoremonger, winebibber, false teacher, false prophet, and many other less-than-desirable titles. He was not guilty of any sin or error, yet in certain seasons the same reasons they celebrated Him, many also hated Him. Your reputation will be called into question multiple times in your life for varying reasons. Your choice to be tenacious in your character and pursuit of accountability through family will be the deciding factor in your capacity to weather the storms of accusation.

Here comes the *confession*! For the sake of the parties mentioned, I will be vague to protect the integrity of all involved. I was in one of the more challenging seasons of my life thus far. I had seen considerable success and failure in my life as far as ministry was concerned. I was a broken man and loved the Lord deeply, my family intensely, and profoundly loved ministry, but still broken. Years of pouring out my soul without proper knowledge of being continually filled by the Spirit of God, coupled with significant relational fractures in my marriage due to the mounting stress of a miscarriage, death of loved ones, and the realities of constant spiritual warfare were coming to a head.

I was burned out, tired of working multiple jobs and only barely able to provide the basics of life. I was exhausted by people acknowledging the anointing of the Lord on my life, and quite frankly, I was tired of hearing the prophetic words over me about going to the nations and influencing others with little to no fruit. The communication between my wife and me was at an all-time low, and I was numb. I was tired of hoping for the impossible or something to happen that may never manifest.

Hope deferred makes the heart sick, but when the desire comes, it is a tree of life (Proverbs 13:12, NKJV).

In retrospect, part of the struggle was our union initiated in a supernatural fashion: dreams, visions, audible voices, and excessive confirmations. But like so many things initiated by the Spirit of God, they would be tested to the core. We were called together, ministered separately, and deeply struggled with how we fit on this level. What made me feel most alive drained my wife to the core and vice versa.

Years of this, among other things, led us to a place where we were just existing. Not thriving, not going backward, just living life the best we knew how. I could feel the resentment when I shared testimonies, stories, or even dreams, but it was the worst thing I could imagine. On the personality spectrum, we are most definitely on opposite ends, so our responses in this season were like throwing a match on gasoline. From the outside looking in, no one would have known, but internally we were about to combust.

Rejection probably has been the most substantial hurdle of my life, consistently taking a considerable, intentional amount of effort to overcome as it arises. A significant part of my story was the lack of mentorship and fathering in ministry, which at this time was a momentous contributor to the situation. To be home was to feel tangible rejection in a way that was suffocating (whether perceived or actual). To be ministering would inevitably lead to a sizeable explosive fight that ended poorly every time. The depths of emotional pain, loneliness, and desperation I was experiencing left me miserable. I found myself on the verge of making an ultimatum with the Lord.

I was going to take a trip that had the possibility of containing a glimmer of hope to see the destiny on my life potentially realized. I told God if He did not do something significant, I was done. No more ministry, no more prophetic function, none of it! If He did not show up for me, I would quit, plain and simple, then get a regular job and live a normal life. Obviously it was the culmination of many things from the flesh to genuine brokenness, desperation, anger, and a laundry list of other issues culminating over time.

As it turns out, God will crash in powerfully whether we deserve it or not. I found myself in a head-on collision with the One who called me, sustained me, broke me, and would now restore me. It's funny how one encounter will recalibrate your perception of the world around you. The problem was, I had experienced a fourteen-day series of encounters, inner healing, fresh filling, and deliverance (a story for another time), and I was headed back into the same environment from where I had so gladly stepped away. I was freshly navigating renewed commitment to the Lord with uncharacteristic naivety. Oh, how reality was about to set in.

It would be a gross overstatement to say that when God calls couples together in marriage and ministry, all of a sudden they synchronize spiritually, emotionally, and physically. However, in Christian culture we have been guilty of making so much about divine encounter moments and never discussing the responsibility of stewarding after those moments.

If you are reading this and are married, you probably recall the series of events that led you and your spouse together as your two lives were drawn together in the holy act of matrimony. If you have been married for any length of time, you are probably thinking, *What the hell happened?*

How can something ordained by heaven feel like hell so quickly? The answer is complicated yet simple. The devil is not standing on the sidelines of your life with pom-poms cheering for you. He is actively opposing you in every area until something starts to work. Family and covenant are the number one weapons of warfare in the global war on Hell. If the devil removes those from society, he wins.

I expected challenges, I expected warfare, but I did not expect it to come like this. When I arrived home, the unsettled issues were not supernaturally resolved in my absence. Much to the contrary, the Lord was visiting my spouse in a much different yet equally abrasive manner. The idea that visitation from the Lord comes without a high price tag is a naïve proposition. Our unique encounters were about to be tested as everything that could be deconstructed in us was deconstructed. Not gently either. The hammer of the Lord is swift, effective, and weighty. The days and months ahead would be filled with tears, brokenness, anger, betrayal, and contrition.

Separation within the context of covenant produces anxiety, accusation, and anger. When walls are constructed through insecurity that covenant was already removed, chaos ensues. For us this resulted in an explosive release of years of pent-up frustration in hideous displays of brokenness. The glory of the Lord exposes everything that needs to be exposed so the blessing of God will not kill you when it comes. Rest assured, you can hide some things for a season, but all will be laid bare before the Lord in due season.

You haven't had real marital trouble until a third party has to be introduced in order to communicate. We were in real danger. Everyone has a breaking point; everyone has their limits, man or woman. I was about to come face-to-face with mine. My wife and I are both extremely strong-willed, which comes with its fair share of fireworks from time to time. The days ahead proved to be like the Fourth of July. Only for us the question would be whether or not these fireworks would have any connection to freedom.

My wife had never been the jealous type. It was one of the qualities I greatly admired and appreciated about her. She never second-guessed my motives, relationships, or intentions. Throughout my ministry (post-infilling of the Holy Spirit), I consistently and regularly worked with or alongside various women in ministry without any issues whatsoever. We operated, fully trusting each other without secrets. Clear protocol, preexisting checks and balances, and the encounter with the Lord were no different on this trip. But somehow it was.

When you experience significant events corporately, frequently a bonding takes place with others involved. You may walk into a room as strangers and leave lifelong friends. The presence of God is like a bonding agent in that regard. During this, I had bonded with several people as we experienced God together. It was a welcome experience to have like-minded believers and friends who generally feel misunderstood and like the oddball.

All of the above considered, when there is a lack of intimacy, communication, and healthy relationship between you and your spouse, all things normal are off the table. In this regard my wife brought up a particular female friend of mine, which irritated me to the core. At first I was hardheaded, angry, and refused to give in on one more thing. In my mind the implication was absurd, preposterous, and outlandish. My stubbornness refused to acknowledge that there was any merit to the implications or even entertain this idea. To add to it, it was nice to have friends.

The pastoral ministry provides you with no shortage of acquaintances and a crazy deficit in legitimate friendships. My unwillingness to acknowledge her concerns and her inability to relent resulted in the most significant impasse of our marriage *to that point*. I do not advise pursuing a deep connection with people when your marriage is in a season of trial. Regardless of your intentions, commitment to your spouse, or spotless history of fidelity, it is not without consequence.

It's important to note that I had no ulterior motives, simply friendship, and it was still not advisable in this season of our lives. When you are hurt and angry, you rarely consider the thoughts and feelings of others. I was guilty in the worst way of disregarding the feelings, trust, and emotions of the one I swore before God to love like Christ loved the church. Wounds unhealed can create a place of neuropathy, and I was numb to all things concerning my marriage at this point. In my brokenness I was unable to hear the more profound ache of my wife's heart. I wanted to be right and justified, after all.

It was not until she went to her mother and two of our closest friends with accusations of an *emotional affair* that I was completely and utterly devastated. Our relationship was undoubtedly in a bad place, but the implication that I would break our covenant to pursue something so frivolous was the most devastating thing I have ever experienced. Stubborn, yes. Insensitive, most definitely. Unfaithful, well, this hurt me in ways words cannot effectively convey. Our disagreements were one thing, but introducing her mother, whom I swore to take care of her daughter when I asked for her hand in marriage, and introducing my two closest friends to the idea that I was involved in infidelity, left me with nothing else to protect.

All of the issues I had tried desperately to keep behind closed doors were now in the open in a way I could not reverse.

You see, my reputation was an idol I was consumed with maintaining. I spent countless hours and much energy supporting the absurd idea that I had everything together and under complete control. Yet in a few moments it came crashing down in a blaze of glory. God is not as concerned with your reputation as you think He is. He is in the restoration business, and He cannot fix what you refuse to acknowledge is broken. You may think the focus of this story is marital reconciliation, but it is not. The unfortunate reality is that regardless of your choice to pursue the Lord through obedience, sacrifice, and the continual process of laying down your life, sometimes you simply fail. *Why* failure happens is not as important as *what* you will do after it has taken place.

There is no feeling less powerless than that of having your entire life and ministry exposed to the elements (and people who may or may not be rooting for you) when you are at your weakest. Most leaders are strong, committed, and devoted to their cause at great expense to themselves. Many would critique this, but years of ministry experience and life lessons learned prove it is sometimes necessary. It is almost an occupational hazard for pioneers blazing new trails and conquering new territory.

The battles you fight will seldom be appreciated, understood, or even acknowledged by those around you. Sometimes you simply have to take one for the team.

However, it is no excuse to *remain* broken, calloused, and indifferent. God is concerned with your character and your heart, dreams, and desires, but He does not care about your reputation. Grasping this reality will allow you to swiftly put any aspirations of great esteem and popularity to death. Something about this life we are called to requires us to die to our reputation so we might come alive in Him.

The unfortunate reality of walking through this broken world is that nothing is guaranteed. As the famous adage goes, "The road to hell is paved with good intentions." I have had the best intentions, solid character, and consistent conduct to end up leaving me in a pile of ashes more times than I can count.

The problem begins when we entertain the idea that our behavior dictates outcomes. Regarding the life of the prophets, this is not accurate. Our behavior stands as a testament to His character and power presently working within us. We have missed the point if we do the right thing for selfish gain or personal benefit. Often you will say the right thing and do the right thing, but your situation will conclude in an unfortunate manner.

I say this not to be discouraging but instead encouraging you that the Lord is not gauging your success based on circumstance and outcomes. He evaluates success based on the internal posture of your heart in the wake of disappointment, irritation, and frustration. Knowing this truth will steady you when everything around you seems to be shaking.

At the risk of inciting significant irritation, I won't tell you how the story ends because it is still in process. That's precisely the point, after all. We are all in process, the good, the bad, and the ugly, all of which belong to Him. Accusation, betrayal, and slander in the life of a prophet are inevitable, but how you respond to this unpleasant reality will in many ways determine how effective your prophetic ministry on this earth will be. Every bit of opposition you experience is an opportunity for the power of Christ in you to be put on display. Opportunities can be seized or missed. Your character, family, and reputation are on top of the devil's hit list. Please don't allow him to gain a foothold that will take you out.

I pray these stories birthed in pain, heartache, disappointment, and brokenness are somehow able to catalyze growth and encouragement in your life. May God grant you the ability to be innocent as doves and wise as a serpent.

4

DEALING WITH THE DOUBLE-MINDED

"People will both embrace and resist you at the same time."

If any of you lacks wisdom, let him ask of God, who gives to all liberally and without reproach, and it will be given to him. But let him ask in faith, with no doubting, for he who doubts is like a wave of the sea driven and tossed by the wind. For let not that man suppose that he will receive anything from the Lord; he is a double-minded man, unstable in all his ways (James 1:5-8, NKJV).

Hypocrisy, the double soul, is destructive, demonic, and confusing in every way and can apply to a prophetic person. Our words and deeds are often merged so that the truth is conveyed regardless of the cost associated. Personally, the merger is problematic publicly because it can quickly become precarious, and privately it often leads to deep anguish. Your ability to understand this part of who you are will in many ways dictate how you navigate life and relationships in every sphere.

Righteous indignation is genuine, rebuke is legal, and reformation takes time. However, how you manage your soul in the process is your responsibility. Grace, mercy, and the razor-thin line between the judgments of God by way of the Word of the Lord are deeply connected to your personhood—the spiritual and the corporeal in human existence; the *imago Dei* that Augustine defined as that principle within us by which we are like God, being able to think and reason, and how we communicate this to other people.

In the case of the prophet, your life is the message. Your gift, call, and anointing are so deeply woven into the fabric of your spirit, soul, and body that it demands you come up higher, even if that means going lower. The weight of this can often feel overwhelming and impossible to navigate. Take heart. He is with you, He is for you, and He is causing all things to work together for the good of those who love Him and are called according to His purpose.

> *These things I have spoken to you, that in Me you may have peace. In the world you will have tribulation; but be of good cheer, I have overcome the world"* (John 16:33, NKJV).

In his book, *Prophetic Ministry*, T. Austin Sparks, a mentor to Watchman Nee and beloved and influenced by many, clarifies one essential point concerning the prophets, "The identity of the vessel with its ministry is the very heart of Divine thought."

STANDING IN THE GAP

Destruction runs rampant where pride is present, and the Lord establishes His prophets as a buffer before judgment is released. Prophets are the first and last line of defense for the body of Christ. However, few are discerning enough to know which warning they are receiving. *Pride goes before destruction, and a haughty spirit before a fall* (Proverbs 16:18, NKJV).

Scripture is filled with references to the destruction connected to ignorance, arrogance, and pride. From the Old Testament to the glorious new covenant in which we now find ourselves, the poison of pride will contaminate the best of intentions. Your gift is powerful, God-given, and divinely empowered through the Spirit of grace to accomplish the purposes of Heaven.

That being said, you must develop an appetite for the Word of God, initiating a transformation of your natural mind in such a way that produces the fruit of the Spirit if you aim to carry any weight or validity in the lives of others. If one aims to stand in the authority and office of a prophet, it is imperative to give yourself to the Scriptures in such a way that your thoughts, intentions, and actions become one and the same.

For the word of God is living and powerful, and sharper than any two-edged sword, piercing even to the division of soul and spirit, and of joints and marrow, and is a discerner of the thoughts and intents of the heart (Hebrews 4:12, NKJV).

Sparks went on to write, "A man is called to represent the thoughts of God, to represent them in what he *is*, not in something that he takes up as a form or line of ministry, not in something that he does. The vessel itself is the ministry, and you cannot divide between the two."

How can one expect to effectively discern the hearts of men and women without first inspecting their hearts in the fear of the Lord? In Matthew 7:3-5, Jesus exhorts them to first remove the plank from their own eye before addressing the dust in the eye of another. Grace is not a license for sin to abound but rather an invitation to ascend higher and raise the bar in declaration and demonstration.

As we increase the input of the Word of God in our lives, interest will accrue based on the deposit made, causing there to be an ample supply of every good thing for every need that may arise in your life.

THE DOUBLE MIND

In James 1:5-8, the author addresses the issues of the double mind, *a double-minded man, unstable in all his ways.* If the Bible is true, and it is, we must learn to set our sight on things above, as Colossians 3 says. Narrowing our focus to the singular lens of Christ and Him crucified is the secret to sustainable Christianity. *If then you were raised with Christ, seek those things, which are above, where Christ is, sitting at the right hand of God. Set your mind on things above, not on things on the earth* (Colossians 3:1-2).

It could be said that any area of your life not submitted to the Word of God and the mind of Christ is under the influence of a demonic, antichrist spirit. It is imperative to cleanse our house and renew our minds through prayer, meditation, and the study of Scriptures. But merely filling our minds with vain, meaningless repetitions is not enough. The house must then be furnished with the thoughts of God and filled with His presence by way of the Holy Spirit. There is simply no substitute. Second Corinthians 3:6 warns us that *the letter kills, but the Spirit gives life.* The Spirit and truth working in unison in our lives are the only things that will produce life, and it's foundational as we pursue His purposes. The singular focus of spirit and truth realized in the person of Jesus Christ is the only way to illuminate your view that you might see clearly.

> Then one was brought to Him who was demon-possessed, blind and mute; and He healed him, so that the blind and mute man both spoke and saw. And all the multitudes were amazed and said, "Could this be the Son of David?" Now when the Pharisees heard it, they said, "This fellow does not cast out demons except by Beelzebub, the ruler of the demons."

> But Jesus knew their thoughts and said to them: *"Every kingdom divided against itself is brought to desolation, and every city or house divided against itself will not stand. If Satan casts out Satan, he is divided against himself. How then will his kingdom stand?* And if I cast out demons by Beelzebub, by whom do your sons cast them out? Therefore they

shall be your judges. But if I cast out demons by the Spirit of God, surely the kingdom of God has come upon you. Or how can one enter a strong man's house and plunder his goods, unless he first binds the strong man? And then he will plunder his house. He who is not with Me is against Me, and he who does not gather with Me scatters abroad" *(Matthew 12:22-30, NKJV, emphasis added).*

But Jesus knew their thoughts— this is never our question. The appropriate question is, do you know His thoughts? Prophets are not designed to sit on fences appeasing the indecisive. Prophets are a stick in the hand of the Lord, drawing a line in the sand, proclaiming, "Choose this day whom you will serve!"

And if it seems evil to you to serve the Lord, choose for yourselves this day whom you will serve, whether the gods which your fathers served that were on the other side of the River, or the gods of the Amorites, in whose land you dwell. But as for me and my house, we will serve the Lord (Joshua 24:15).

His thoughts do not waver from left to right or shift with the seasons. He is constant, He is fixed, and He does not change. As prophetic representatives of the oracles of God, our character, actions, and heart posture must mirror the One we claim to represent. Conflict is inevitable; how you handle it is up to you.

And the spirits of the prophets are subject to the prophets (1 Corinthians 14:32, NKJV). Very seldom do we hear this Scripture in the context of personal prophetic responsibility. Without digging too deeply into theological constructs or depths of spiritual principles, it would be safe to say that God does not give you a gift, call, or anointing without the ability to steward your life well. It does not mean that it will not come with its fair share of challenges. The challenges are not an excuse to opt out of life reflecting the character of Christ. Contrary to popular belief, your gift does not carry with it an exemption for personal responsibility. Sensitivity, betrayal, warfare, and heartache, while a reality, are not an opportunity to shift the subject or change the narrative.

A DOUBLE-MINDED PROPHET

What does a double-minded prophet look like? It is a question worth asking. If you are trusted with rightly dividing the Word of truth, conveying the prophetic proclamations that shape nations, and rebuking the saints when necessary, then we must come up higher by embracing our call to holiness.

If we are not vigilant, we run the risk of sliding down the slippery slope of accusation, condemnation, and judgments that do not reflect the heart of the Father. Matthew 6:22 reminds us that *the lamp of the body is the eye. If therefore your eye is good, your whole body will be full of light* (NKJV).

I propose that prophets develop double vision before they reach the place of being double-minded. The moment our eyes shift from the place of affection, adoration, and acknowledging the beauty of Christ, we forget the place from where our authority is seated.

I am reminded of the emphatic words echoed by the author in Hebrews 12:1-2, *Therefore we also, since we are surrounded by so great a cloud of witnesses, let us lay aside every weight, and the sin which so easily ensnares us, and let us run with endurance the race that is set before us, looking unto Jesus, the author and finisher of our faith, who for the joy that was set before Him endured the cross, despising the shame, and has sat down at the right hand of the throne of God* (NKJV).

What is the essence and face of enduring love? How do we model healthy prophetic ministry in a way that reflects the heart of the Father? We must first recognize that the ministry of reconciliation is our primary mandate. While there are many prophetic objectives, seasonal words, and specific directives that emerge as the vein of prophetic ministry, the love of the Father in the face of the Son is paramount.

Therefore, if anyone is in Christ, he is a new creation; old things have passed away; behold, all things have become new. Now all things are of God, who has reconciled us to Himself through Jesus Christ, and has given us the ministry of reconciliation, that is, that God was in Christ reconciling the world to Himself, not imputing their trespasses to them, and has committed to us the word of reconciliation. Now then, we are ambassadors for Christ, as though God were pleading through us: we implore you on Christ's behalf, be reconciled to God. For He made Him who knew no sin to be sin for us, that we might become the righteousness of God in Him (2 Corinthians 5:17-21, NKJV).

The very purpose of the sacrificial atonement through the death of Jesus on the cross was forgiveness, redemption, and reconciliation through the precious blood of Jesus. How can one stand in the name of the Lord declaring condemnation and final judgment when the very foundation of the good news of the Gospel opposes this ideology? We must lock into this eternal reality that our primary function as messengers of the oracles of the Lord is to convey the eternal Gospel in a way that releases hope-filled solutions for hopeless people.

When human emotions are ascribed to God, the pathos of God, such as grief, wrath, and love, must be mirrored in our lives, never being *apathetic but always passionately concerned.*

Even His judgments concerning sin and compromise are redemptive in that they bring about discipline that results in lasting transformation. While He is the same yesterday, today, and forever, His involvement in our lives is uniquely and distinctly personal. For the prophets, this requires clean hands and a pure heart that we might rightly discern the word of the Lord in our respective spheres of influence. In summary, we cannot allow the circle of double-mindedness around us to produce double-mindedness in us.

As you pursue a pure expression of prophetic demonstration in your life, I encourage you to fix your gaze on the person of Jesus Christ so you cannot help but see the goodness of God overshadowing the plans of the enemy. In the good and bad things in life and the happy and sad, God holds the final word. May you plumb new depths in the heart of God and reach new heights in the mind of Christ.

> Let this mind be in you which was also in Christ Jesus, who, being in the form of God, did not consider it robbery to be equal with God, but made Himself of no reputation, taking the form of a bondservant, and coming in the likeness of men. And being found in appearance as a man, He humbled Himself and became obedient to the point of death, even the death of the cross *(Philippians 2:5-8, NKJV).*

5

STRENGTHEN YOURSELF IN THE LORD

"Your office is a GIFT to you AND those around you."

Now David was greatly distressed, for the people spoke of stoning him, because the soul of all the people was grieved, every man for his sons and his daughters. **But David strengthened himself in the LORD his God** *(1 Samuel 30:6, NKJV, emphasis added).*

G rief, distress, and the trials of life are enough to bring you to the end of yourself. Somehow in our minds we have a way of fantasizing about a one-time completed work of death and consecration to the Lord. As much as I wish it were true, it simply isn't. The longer we operate under this false presupposition, the more unnecessary heartache we will endure under a fog of disillusionment. In my life, the inevitability of this reality resulted in what feels like a never-ending wrestling match with the purposes of God. A love-hate relationship; love for the benefits, and distain for the price tag associated with the high call of friendship with the Creator.

Then He said to them all, "If anyone desires to come after Me, let him deny himself, and take up his cross daily, and follow Me. For whoever desires to save his life will lose it, but whoever loses his life for My sake will save it (Luke 9:23-24, NKJV).

DON'T RESIST, EMBRACE THE PROCESS

The invitation to resurrection power is a veiled invitation to the cross. It is a daily death that can result in a daily resurrection and divine empowerment doing what you are incapable of in your own strength. There is no sacrifice to put on the altar apart from death; there is no resurrection life apart from death. Its inevitability is an absolute in the Christian life. Security and predictability are not part of the package. The longer you choose to believe this vain imagination, the more you are surprised when facing uncertainty, trials, tribulation, and opposition. Patient endurance produces in us patient endurance and wisdom that will stand the test of time.

My brethren, count it all joy when you fall into various trials, knowing that the testing of your faith produces patience. But let patience have its perfect work, that you may be perfect and complete, lacking nothing. If any of you lacks wisdom, let him ask of God, who gives to all liberally and without reproach, and it will be given to him (James 1:2-5, NKJV).

Persecution is promised, betrayal and slander are in the fine print, and rejection is a reality you will face in varying degrees all the days of your life. The sooner you embrace this, the less time you will spend mourning the loss of something that was never yours in the beginning. The fellowship of His sufferings qualifies you to take these tests in the same manner Jesus did. After all, the Holy Spirit led Jesus into the wilderness to be tested by the devil (Matthew 4:1). This same Jesus came to His own, and His own knew Him not (John 1:11). It is part of a process that refines us in our spirit, body, and soul. The refiner's fire burns in a way not adequately articulated; it requires experiential knowledge for proper understanding to be grasped.

If incapable of grasping the foundational truths and elementary understandings of the prophetic role and function, we will find ourselves in a perpetual state of condemnation. The idea that some consider death, rejection, and suffering due to failure will cripple a prophet. In actuality, most times they are confirmation you are moving in the direction of Christ. It is not a matter of if, but when. Yes, it hurts like hell, but the result will be heaven's manifestation on earth if you stay the course! Embrace your cross, suffer well, and take time to fully embrace the process that is perfecting you from glory to glory. George Mueller, a man of great faith, said, "If we desire our faith to be strengthened, we should not shrink from opportunities where our faith may be tried, and therefore, through trial, be strengthened."

STRENGTH FROM WEAKNESS

How can one glean strength from weakness? How do I move from ashes to beauty? The answer is in Paul's words to the church at Corinth when he wrote that *for the sake of Christ, then, I am content with weaknesses, insults, hardships, persecutions, and calamities. For when I am weak, then I am strong* (2 Corinthians 12:10, ESV). In Paul's introduction to spiritual weapons, he wrote to the church and Ephesus, *as to the rest, my brethren, be strengthened in the Lord, and in the strength of his power.* (Ephesians 6:10, SLT).

In his book, *Strengthen Yourself in the Lord*, Bill Johnson wrote, "I have purposed to try to live in such a way that nothing ever gets bigger than my consciousness of God's presence." Bill makes it clear that the renewing of the mind is key to strengthening yourself in the Lord. "Your faith grows as your heart, led by the Holy Spirit, perceives and understands the invisible realm of spiritual reality. That unseen realm governs the visible realm and brings your mind and will into an agreement with the reality of the Kingdom. In essence, what I have just described is the process of renewing the mind."

David said that the Lord is our strength, and if we do not learn how to strengthen ourselves in the Lord, we will fail to live a fruitful, powerful, and meaningful life. While this may sound harsh, it is a wake-up call for those who would aim to call themselves messengers of God. God's choosing you and calling you will invite all manner of opposition from every imaginable side, never imagining the opposition and hurdles you will face in life.

REALIGNING YOUR PERCEPTIONS AND PRIORITIES

It is easy to live at the mercy of profound encounters and spiritual experiences while presuming that the height of their spirituality is the floor of the prophetic process. It may sound arrogant or insensitive, but this false view of the prophetic process is an unfortunate reality for man. The reason is that many individuals fail to develop the strength of mind and courage to the course and contend for the prophetic destiny God intended. Strengthening yourself in the Lord implies a personal responsibility to steward the gift, calling, and anointing on your life as a logical act of service.

Within the prophetic community it rarely emphasizes free will, the freedom to make decisions, and the invitation to wisdom. There is profuse focus on the word of the Lord, prophetic future, and what is happening in the spiritual realm. Such overemphasis in these areas will create a massive imbalance with real and lasting implications. Unhealthy cycles are destined to repeat themselves until they are broken through a conscious act of the will.

What I wrote in an earlier paragraph, I knew it was a radical statement with intense inferences: "Many live their lives at the mercy of encounters and experiences, as the height of their spirituality is the floor of the prophetic process." So for the sake of those who might not understand, I will provoke your thoughts a bit more.

One week in the life of those called to the office of a prophet may contain more supernatural experiences, dreams, visions, and encounters than the average believer can capture in a lifetime. All these supernatural experiences can be authentic, yet the walls surrounding you can still collapse upon your spiritual gift.

The attack on your soul will not relent only because of your deep spiritual connections. Do not mistake spiritual experiences for intimacy with Jesus. While there may be spiritual connectivity at different points in your life, your ability to separate and distinguish intimacy from intuition will decide the righteous consistency of your life and ministry.

Responsibility and authority go hand in hand. The monumental weight of stewarding the glory of the Lord by way of prophetic revelation is no joke. Our willingness to engage while wrestling through the process of bringing our thoughts and emotions in submission to the heart of the Father is paramount. The ability to strengthen yourself in the Lord when your inner circle dissolves, family walks away, and mockers gather around the glorious spectacle of your life is the difference between life and death.

I remember the words of the disciples after Jesus exercised His definition of crowd control by teaching on the necessity of eating His flesh and drinking His blood (John 6:54). He had just miraculously fed the five thousand through the multiplication of the loaves and the fishes, walked on water, and now cannibalism. It was as if one of Jesus' favorite pastimes was gathering a massive following and then offending the hell out of them. Dazed and confused in the aftermath of this PR nightmare, with many reevaluating their decision to follow this Jesus of

Nazareth, the disciples entered into this dialogue for which I am eternally grateful.

> From that time many of His disciples went back and walked with Him no more. Then Jesus said to the twelve, ***"Do you also want to go away?"*** But Simon Peter answered Him, "Lord, to whom shall we go? You have the words of eternal life" *(John 6:66-68, NKJV, emphasis added)*.

If there was ever a narrative that has played out in my head consistently over my years of walking with Jesus, this is it. After much prayer, intercession, consistency, and pursuit of this Jesus, He goes and says something that utterly destroys my grid for reality. Just when I feel like I have figured it out, or at least have a grasp on what is expected, Jesus Himself throws a wrench in the whole thing. "Jesus, this is a hard statement to accept!" His reply, short and to the point, "Are you going to leave Me?" to which I respond, "Where else can I go? Your words are everything to me!" (John 6:60-70).

The bitter and the sweet, the grace and the severity, the offense and the mercy all come from the mouth of Jesus. Not only His words but also His very essence is the manifestation of the heart of the Father towards humanity! Not only are His words life, but also His actions and the thought process behind them. He is the literal culmination and manifestation of heaven's intent for humanity.

> *And the Word became flesh and dwelt among us, and we beheld His glory, the glory as of the only begotten of the Father, full of grace and truth (John 1:14, NKJV).*

I believe the problem for most remains in our definition or estimation of strength. In the garden of Gethsemane, Jesus was in essence strengthening Himself for the task ahead. Sweating drops of blood in the natural, He brings His will into submission to the purposes of God for His life by no other means than listening to the voice of the Father. The admonition found in Hebrews is a key to laying hold of what it means to strengthen ourselves in the Lord. *For consider Him who endured such hostility from sinners against Himself, lest you become weary and discouraged in your souls. You have not yet resisted to bloodshed, striving against sin* (Hebrews 12:3-4, NKJV).

So the question is, have you resisted unto bloodshed and travailed over the destiny of your life in the wee hours of the morning while on the brink of betrayal, humiliation, and public execution?

It is there and only there, where you develop the internal resolve required to run the race to completion and lay hold of the prize, which is the full measure of Jesus. It has nothing to do with your ability and everything to do with running into the name of the Lord, which is a strong tower where the righteous find refuge.

For He made Him who knew no sin to be sin for us, that we might become the righteousness of God in Him (2 Corinthians 5:21, NKJV).

The only way to strengthen yourself *in* the Lord is retreating into the finished work of the cross. Connection, communion, and unity with the Son through the mind of Christ and the power of the Spirit are both the foundation and the pinnacle of this upside-down Kingdom in which we find ourselves. The way to ascend is to descend, lowering yourself in humility, suffering long, and dying honorably, but death on a cross is the doorway to resurrection life.

This is the unfortunate reality for those who choose to remain steadfast, but you will stand alone on the Word of the Lord at some point. Friends, family, ministry partners, and people you never dreamed would abandon you will disappear in some of the most challenging seasons of your life. In extreme circumstances, they will not only desert you but also oppose and question your motives.

The pain is real, excruciating, and refining. Rejection is difficult, accusations are awful, but in the process you have the unique ability to bring clarity to relationships, existing realities, and unnecessary hindrances. It also reminds us of who our Source is, where we find comfort, and the place in which we find our identity and purpose.

When embraced, these perpetual cycles of pruning, purging, and purification lend themselves to dependency rather than strength. That's just it! In this topsy-turvy Kingdom , weakness equals strength, which is a major key when attempting to strengthen yourself in the Lord. It means that you lean into the pain as it purifies you in your pursuit of intimacy with the Trinity. The word strength is predicated on the understanding that separation equals incapacitation while union means strength. The degree that we link ourselves to the suffering, sacrifice, death, and burial of Jesus is to the degree we will experience resurrection power.

6

PROPHET IS NOT A GREEK WORD FOR "HARD TO GET ALONG WITH"

"No one will ever receive the prophetic when released in pride!"

Stubborn, hardheaded, dogmatic, immovable, impossible, unrealistic—these are just a few of the things I have been called over the years. In the beginning my unbridled passion for truth, justice, and the recompense of God could be likened to an intoxicated friend unable to keep their observations and emotions to themselves, constantly vomiting their strong opinions on others. In other words, it created a lot of problems for me.   Concerning the prophetic, God does not wait until you are mature before releasing the weight of the call on your life. Its burden shapes you, molds you, and tempers you until you mirror what the Father saw before time began; healthy, whole, confident, and secure in our identity in Christ. It is imperative to take the necessary time to deal with the areas of the soul, the flesh, and unsettled disappointments in your life lest they contaminate our prophetic utterance all the days of our lives.

My goal is not to discourage you from expressing deep emotion, strong empathetic unction, passionate pursuit of justice, and strong desire to see reform manifest in the earth. I would, however, challenge you to harness those elements by concentrating on an intentional release of calculated words released in due season. Due season is the goal and being able to discern the times and seasons separates the seasoned prophets from the wannabe messengers, unwilling to endure the process that qualifies them to release the words of God that first shape them. *And let us not grow weary while doing good, for in due season we shall reap if we do not lose heart* (Galatians 6:9, NKJV).

Over time weariness saps your strength, compromises your clarity, and distorts your discernment until you begin to question everything. It is vital that you revisit, remember, and retrace your steps prophetically in times like this. Honesty is the best policy when dealing with issues of the heart. An honest evaluation of what God said, what you heard, and what went wrong will allow you to crucify your flesh, rip apart vain imaginations, and reconcile unfortunate realities you discovered above your reach.

I can hear the reader pondering, "What are you saying, Justin? What does this have to do with being difficult to work with me? In essence, I would say that your prophetic tendencies and intuitive disposition are not excuses to negate growing in compassion, sensitivity, and understanding. *Prophet* is not a Greek word for *'hard to get along with!'* "

PAIN OF THE PROPHET

You have been given a gift, a divine opportunity, to significantly impact the world around you by releasing radical hope and transformation. Prophets are predisposed to more rejection than most due to the nature of their position and function. But this reality does not negate the call to take up your cross and follow Him. Born crucified, so you no longer live, which is painful; it is a process as Christ emerges within you (Galatians 2:20).

The presence of pain does not remove the great need for a proactive pursuit of purpose. In the Kingdom, pain is never pointless but always valuable if you don't resist. While God may not be the author of it, He will most definitely use it for our good and somehow create a favorable outcome for those who claim His name and walk in His ways. The moment you elevate your prophetic ability to see, hear, and feel above God's ability to free, heal, and restore, you have grossly miscalculated your need for heart reconstruction.

One of the unique conundrums is when prophets are probably correct most of the time. But just because you have the right information does not mean your heart is settled in His redemptive purposes concerning that information. Discernment is tricky; it can identify a currently existing problem without seeing its future direction. Prophets tune in to a person's motive, compromise, and sin because the purpose of that particular gift is to separate good and evil, right and wrong, and between better and best. While it is imperative to possess the ability to identify wrong from right, the prophetic act is a redemptive tool in which we bridge the gap between current reality and a hopeful future. Here is the kicker: prophets are given a measure of authority through the redemptive work of Calvary that activates us as ambassadors for Christ, enabling us to make judgments through our declarations foretelling a redemptive future. If we rely too heavily on discernment while negating the work of the cross, we exercise authority incorrectly and potentially put people in bondage instead of launching them into their destiny.

Prophets must mirror Christ so closely that they become irresistible to the world around them, life-giving solutionists that carry heaven's DNA! What if the judgments the prophetic community is known for were so redemptive that the lost were found, sinners became saints, and the broken made whole? But a challenge exists because the devil knows the measure of authority and weight of the words on the prophet's shoulder. The devil knows this and will not relent in his efforts to discourage, delay, and defame those operating in this glorious gift from heaven.

PROPHETS OF HOPE

If the powers of darkness effectively blockade hope in the prophets' lives, their hearts will grow sick. A heartsick prophet can be an instrument of death rather than a catalyst for life because the mouth speaks from the heart's overflow. I argue that if the hopeful expectation of the prophets is compromised, the whole church could quickly spiral out of control because the anchor to our soul is Christ.

Being fully human, Christ was filled with the Holy Spirit, tested at all points, and possessing the keys, both the rightful and the actual dominion over death and hell. The first and the last, the living One was dead but now lives forever possessing the keys. It is fascinating that in the following verse, Jesus says, *Write the things which you have seen, and the things which are, and the things which will take place after this* (Revelation 1:19, NKJV). Notice the prophetic prescription for healing the church is by delivering spiritual insight concerning the present condition and then contributing foresight into the future healing which gives hope.

The soul includes the mind, will, and emotions, the intangible medium of human expression, but in the emptiness of the darkened mind, alienated from God's life, and lacking spiritual knowledge because of the hardening of the heart (Ephesians 4:17, paraphrase). Jesus had to overcome the fundamental flaws and pitfalls of the human condition by the power of the Spirit, which is the only thing that can heal and keep us steady in the storms of life. Christ is our only hope for stabilizing the soul.

*This **hope** we have as an **anchor of the soul**, both sure and steadfast, and which enters the Presence behind the veil, where the forerunner has entered for us, even Jesus, having become High Priest forever according to the order of Melchizedek (Hebrews 6:19-20, emphasis added).*

This hope is not like the world gives, but rather it is a concrete foundation built on the One where we entered into death, burial, *and* resurrection with Him. It is not a wishing well where we toss our letters of hopes and wishes or one whispered hope as we watch a shooting star disappear into the dark canvas of the night sky. This hope is an invitation to the glory that Christ walked in as a human on this earth. As one with Christ, we are invited to move in the same exploits, challenges, victories, and heartaches, rejection, and hostilities. *To them God willed to make known what are the riches of the glory of this mystery among the Gentiles:which is* **Christ in you**, *the* **hope of glory** (Colossians 1:27, NKJV, emphasis added).

This revelation of Christ in you as the hope of glory is the answer to what plagues humanity. The portending question is whether or not you will be a harbinger of hope or a disciple of death. Choice in the abundance of options is a powerful yet ominous thing.

The heart of the Father is not to remove options but to equip and empower you to make the best choices despite the riptides pulling you away. God wants to add weight to your account through a deposit of His glory so you can do all things possible to stand against anything the world, the flesh, or the devil throws at you.

FREEDOM OF WILL

The human free will is revealed throughout Scripture, clearly indicating God gives us choices and calls us to choose the way the Father knows best. See, I set before you today life and prosperity, death and destruction. For

I command you today to love the Lord your God, walk in His ways, then you will live and surge forward, but if your heart turns away and you are not obedient to God, you will self-destruct (see Deuteronomy 30).

The free will anchored in divine destiny and identity is a recipe for breakthrough! It is time for the sons and daughters to move from a lifestyle of obligation created by guilt, shame, and condemnation to a lifestyle of invitation to ascend to a higher plane of existence. Jesus paid the price so you could live freely and shamelessly, the ultimate destination for the saints! The blueprints of Eden contained a garden with not one but two trees! Life in Eden's garden offered options and the freedom to choose based on godly discernment, or the other option that leads to catastrophe and exclusion.

Religion, absent from the Spirit of God, is nothing more than a series of checks and balances that will ultimately suck the life out of you. While there is much to be said for doing the right thing regardless of how you may or may not feel about it, that ideology can be problematic if it becomes the norm. This transformation process is much different from conformation; one is active, while the other is passive.

TRAINING THE MIND

You've heard it said that a mind is a terrible thing to waste. I would propose that for a believer, the definition of wasting your mind would be neglecting to *proactively* take every thought captive and bring it into submission to the mind of Christ. Science would now back up the importance of training your brain. Your brain can learn and grow as you age—a process called brain plasticity—but you have to train it regularly for it to do so.

Mere intellect will not dismantle deeply rooted errors in your thinking. Changing the way you think changes your perspective, which changes how you act in the world. Paul's words reflect how to retrain the brain. *And we pull down reasonings and every high thing that is exalted against the knowledge of God, and we take all minds prisoner to the obedience of The Messiah* (2 Corinthians 10:5, Aramaic Bible in Plain English).

Paul's words in 2 Corinthians 10 aren't new. "Change your mind" is the central theme of Jesus' first sermon (Matthew 4:17). *From then on, Jesus began to tell people, "Turn to God and change the way you think and act, because the kingdom of heaven is near"* (GW).

It is not a mindless series of actions but rather a conscious, intentional process of engaging a course of action to build with God in a way that fortifies our minds against the tricks and wiles of the enemy.

DYNAMICS OF TRUST

Trust implies that though we do not yet understand the process or reasoning behind it, we have faith in the one administering the instructions and has our best interest at heart. Trust empowers us to let go of our strong desires, opinions, and need for control, thus enabling us to release the word of the Lord, absent from the negative imprints of the world around us.

If you are incapable of grasping this on a genuine and personal level, our effectiveness with other systems, structures, and personalities will be severely impaired. Pride is bound to manifest when presumption becomes the lens through which we view the revelation crossing our line of spiritual sight. Dogma and discernment are not necessarily synonymous. Trust is the catalyst that allows the prophet to yield their mind, will, and emotions as well as their natural intellect to the word of the Lord. It is not attained through your gift or achieved through a fight. Trust is displayed through submission, patient endurance, and meekness. Authority is modeled through confidence that transcends methods, models, percentages, and probabilities.

Resolve, endurance, and longsuffering in their proper context will break a person's will, desires, and selfish disposition. But if a seasoned prophet is prideful, they more than likely have issues of disobedience, disappointment, or delusions. While you will most definitely wrestle with the shortsightedness of those around you throughout your prophetic journey, your role and function are not to be served but to serve.

It is your job to work with those who cannot see and hear until they can perceive in a manner that speaks in the Father's tone. Good teachers are not self-centered, self-serving, or self-focused. If you find yourself in a place of resentment, take a break, take stock internally, and get the healing you need to effectively minister the gospel of reconciliation. Ephesians 4 is our mandate, equipping the saints for the work of ministry. The call is specific, the result is redemptive, and the ministry nonnegotiable.

Young prophet, direct the deep tension, conflict, and the resilience inside you towards powers, principalities, and wickedness in high places. Make no mistake, for your disposition is ordered of the Lord, your destiny unquestioned. Still, your decision to proactively contend for compassion towards humanity is equally impactful in the grand scheme of things.

Allow the breaking to keep you moldable, pliable, and ultimately sensitive to the heart of the Father. We *do not* wrestle against flesh and blood. Your enemy is not your brother, sister, father, mother, or neighbor. It is imperative to establish it at the very core of your being so when demonic storms disorient you and destroy the house God is building in your life, your foundation remains immovable. Your decision to yield to the Holy Spirit dictates the scale and scope of prophetic assignments you are entrusted with throughout your life. Remember, prophets are servants, messengers, and ministers of reconciliation. You were born for this!

7

BE HUMBLE

"Humility encourages honor."

The fear of the LORD is the instruction of wisdom And before honor is humility (Proverbs 15:33, NKJV).

Humility is the heart posture of the sons and daughters of God. Before I am a prophet, I am a son; before I am a prophet, I am a sinner saved by grace through faith in Jesus Christ. The constant connection to this reality of who we are and being implanted in the soil of the good news of the Gospel of the Kingdom allows us to have roots going deep into Him. The deeper the roots, the greater the fruit. There are lessons learned as we walk in humility that cannot be found in any other area of life. There is a pressing, squeezing, and crushing that can only be experienced as we humble ourselves under the hand of the Lord and to the world around us. Only a person who has passed through the gate of humility can ascend to the heights of the spirit (Rudolph Steiner).

But he who is greatest among you shall be your servant. And whoever exalts himself will be humbled, and he who humbles himself will be exalted (Matthew 23:11-12, NKJV).

Scripture's theme on humility highlights the importance of willful submission and surrender under God's hand. *Humble yourselves under the mighty hand of God so that He may exalt you at the proper time* (1 Peter 5:6, NASB). The capacity to proactively initiate acts of service in an attitude of humility that ultimately leads to advancement and exaltation is profound. Capturing and adopting this principle early in your prophetic journey will position you favorably in your journey towards the destiny God has set before you.

While I do not believe you can speed up the process the Lord has placed you in your life, you can most definitely slow it down. Among the list of things that are detrimental to apprehending your destiny, disobedience will stop you dead in your tracks. I have watched anointed believers that have resisted the ministry of humility get stuck in needless cycles of humiliation, failure, and dead ends, refusing to bend their will in the season the Lord had placed them.

In the case of a prophet, disobedience is rooted in the deceptive lie that you know better than God. It is a subtle yet effective tactic of the enemy to get you to take control of your life rather than submitting under the mighty hand of the Lord. The drive to extract yourself from the space that causes discomfort or pain is a natural inclination. One could argue that prophets' capacity to submit their will to the Lord when facing intense opposition is as supernatural as the exploits ascribed to the prophetic office.

HUMILITY IS A VIRTUE BUT PAINFUL

At its core, humility is the intentional restraint of radical power and should not be confused with low self-esteem, self-degradation, or a lack of value for one's life. When applied to life on the altar, humility is a sweet-smelling aroma in the nostrils of the Lord. Grasping your identity in Christ and the created value revealed through the sacrifice of Jesus on the cross, everything changes. The access to authority we have as sons and daughters of God is never in question, but the remaining question remaining is, what will we do with that authority? If the testimony of Jesus is the spirit of prophecy and in these last days God has spoken through His Son, then it would be wise to defer to Christ.

Let this mind be in you which was also in Christ Jesus, who, being in the form of God, did not consider it robbery to be equal with God, but made Himself of no reputation, taking the form of a bondservant, and coming in the likeness of men. And being found in appearance as a man, He humbled Himself and became obedient to the point of death, even the death of the cross. Therefore God also has highly exalted Him and given Him the name which is above every name, that at the name of Jesus every knee should bow, of those in heaven, and of those on earth, and of those under the earth, and that every tongue should confess that Jesus Christ is Lord, to the glory of God the Father (Philippians 2:5-11, NKJV).

Authority is never the question, but how we exercise it is always the issue. Jesus was the Son of God, the incarnation of the Trinity, taking the form of a human, fully God and fully man. Nothing would change who He is, the Son of God. However, His willful act to take the form of a bondservant, humbling Himself, and dying to man's opinions regarding His identity empowered Him to break people out of a system that was poisoning their perspective. They had their uninspired ideas while Jesus bore the image of God.

God, who at various times and in various ways spoke in time past to the fathers by the prophets, has in these last days spoken to us by His Son, whom He has appointed heir of all things, through whom also He made the worlds; who being the brightness of His glory and the express image of His person, and upholding all things by the word of His power, when He had by Himself purged our sins, sat down at the right hand of the Majesty on high, having become so much better than the angels, as He has by inheritance obtained a more excellent name than they (Hebrews 1:1-4, NKJV).

The brightness of God's glory and the express image of His person clothed Himself with humility rather than hostility to manifest the message of His Kingdom coming and His will be done. The message of death is seldom celebrated, rarely received, and often ignored. Consequently, the ministry of reconciliation with which the prophets have been entrusted is infrequently demonstrated. Genuine prophetic voices are first obedient sons and daughters. If Jesus Himself grew in obedience, you and I could most definitely learn a thing or two by following Jesus. *Though He was a Son, yet He learned obedience by the things which He suffered* (Hebrews 5:8, NKJV).

A PLACE ONLY ACQUIRED THROUGH HUMILITY

If there were ever a passage I despised, wrestled with, and walked away from at times, it would most definitely be that verse. The idea that identity is secure in sonship yet your position is acquired through humble acts of submission to the will is a stellar example of opposite truths held in tension. The natural mind insists these two ideologies have to be at odds with each other. However, the Spirit of God both expects and demands the impossible.

I believe my fundamental struggle rests in where I fall between the two . You see, I am practical and might even argue logically if the opportunity presented itself. My logical mind often works to my disadvantage concerning matters of the heart. When it comes to humility, it is counterintuitive, countercultural, and a statistically improbable means of advancement.

If I were to follow that train of thought down the track in front of me, I would eventually find myself processing my life in a linear reality, measuring success by movement rather than motives. The perspective looking through that lens lends itself to a beginning, middle, and end model. But His lens is not logically fixed as humans, for God's lens sits outside of time, space, and every human limitation. The One who imagined you into existence watches over the words that created the world in which you live. And He causes all things to work together for the good of those who love Him and are called according to His purpose.

HUMILITY OF DEATH

Suffering has a purifying quality for those who will yield to its work in their life. It is a truth that strength and fortitude are not revealed until they meet resistance. And that being true, then the inferior structures of pride must crumble under the weight of glory so God can breathe on the dust of death and contrition, causing beauty to rise from ashes and death to be swallowed up by resurrection power. After all, that is the ultimate goal.

The prophetic words carry the same weight as God's authority and power that bind the forces of hell and loose the reality of heaven on earth. The prophetic ministry has nothing to do with your ego, reputation, or public image; it has everything to do with the heart and intent of the Father being released on the earth. However, the eternal message of the cross will not be avoided, averted, or overlooked in the life and message of any genuine prophet. You will die a thousand deaths if your ministry carries any weight whatsoever. When you think you are done, the process will begin again, refining the parts of you that are at enmity with the God, who wants to bless and prosper you.

Have you ever wondered why Jesus died such a gruesome, rigorous, and public death on a cross of all things? Imagine being fastened to an immovable object and forced to endure a slow, humiliating, and painful death. I have heard preachers give multiple answers, inserting their perspective on this subject. Why couldn't it be swift, some would question? But there is something about pain that is purifying, clarifying, and magnifying. It purifies our imperfections, defines our purpose, and magnifies the message that must come through us to others.

> *He is despised and rejected by men, A Man of sorrows and acquainted with grief. And we hid, as it were, our faces from Him; He was despised, and we did not esteem Him. Surely, He has borne our griefs and carried our sorrows; Yet we esteemed Him stricken, Smitten by God, and afflicted* (Isaiah 53:3-4, NKJV).

We often sterilize the Gospel's message in such a way that separates the life and ministry of Christ from the lives of you and me. And somehow we assume that the statement of Jesus on the cross as He commits His spirit into the hands of the Father, saying, "It is finished!" would imply that we are finished. The cross is an invitation into the fullness of all Jesus made accessible to us! It would be essential to note that the ways of God and the nature of Jesus are one and the same. This passage is astounding!

> *Yet it pleased the LORD to bruise (crush) Him; He has put Him to grief. When You make His soul an offering for sin, He shall see His seed, He shall prolong His days, And the pleasure of the LORD shall prosper in His hand. He shall see the labor of His soul and be sat-*

isfied. By His knowledge My righteous Servant shall justify many, For He shall bear their iniquities (Isaiah 53:10-11, NKJV, emphasis added).

KNOWLEDGE OF THE GLORY

One of the often-overlooked effects of humility through the process of humiliation is the redemptive nature it has for those we are proactively directing it. Humility by nature appears to be a detriment to the one operating in it. It is a spiritual principle to kick against the systems of this world. It is not natural and often unmerited for those who are most necessary to extend towards them. As prophets, our refusal to operate in this spiritual principle is the difference between life and death. In other words, the question, "Is it worth it?" is all relative to the individual on the brink of death and destruction. Our Good Shepherd is the One who leaves the ninety-nine to chase after the one that has lost their way. As far as the Kingdom is concerned, denial of self is the beginning of true prosperity.

*Then Jesus said to His disciples, "If anyone desires to come after Me, **let him deny himself**, and take up his cross, and follow Me. For whoever desires to save his life will lose it, but whoever loses his life for My sake will find it. (Matthew 16:24-25, NKJV, emphasis added).*

In Habakkuk 2:14, the prophet painted a prophetic picture of the last days, when the earth will be filled with the knowledge of the glory as the waters cover the sea. The suffering, glory, and reconciliation of humanity are all interwoven together. The value of an item is determined by the price willing to be paid for ownership.

God the Father set the fair market value for humanity when He saw fit to exchange His Son, the lamb slain from the foundation of the world, as a ransom for the redemption of humankind. Somehow the humiliation of the man Christ Jesus is key to riches and honor.

By humility and the fear of the LORD Are riches and honor and life (Proverbs 22:4, NKJV).

Humble yourselves in the sight of the Lord, and He will lift you up (James 4:10, NKJV).

Therefore, humble yourselves under the mighty hand of God, that He may exalt you in due time, casting all your care upon Him, for He cares for you (1 Peter 5:6-7, NKJV).

"Honor encourages honor."

Dating back to Eden's garden, fruitfulness is inseparable from the Kingdom mandate, which was to be
fruitful, multiply, fill the earth, and subdue it. It was not
solely for populating the earth but a perpetual word of
ensuring cycles of seed, time, and harvest. It is true natu-
rally, spiritually, relationally, and the list continues. Fruitfulness and faithfulness are attached to the original mandate. Faithfulness and fruitfulness must not be divided
because they are the twin towers of a life pleasing to God.

*Let a man so consider us, as servants of Christ and
stewards of the mysteries of God. Moreover it is required in stewards that one be found faithful (1 Corinthians 4:1-2, NKJV).*

What is faithfulness? What does it look like to steward the words of God? How about our time? What is my
role in the harvest? All of these are thoughts we will ex-
plore throughout our journey as faithful stewards of

God's promises. Fruitfulness involves your decision to be faithful through the good times and the bad. The winter seasons and those of fall are equally important as the spring and summer. *To everything there is a season, A time for every purpose under heaven* (Ecclesiastes 3:1, NKJV). Every season is one of receding, but not always one of rising; one of seedtime, but not always harvest. During the ebbs and flow of life, our ability to embrace the purposes of God determines its results.

Seeds are words and words are seeds, and in the case of the prophet it cannot be overstated. So if the command is fruitfulness, then we must understand the power of the seeds with which the Lord entrusts us. The ability to discern the proper soil, suitable season, and intended setting will often determine the seed's life. It also provides insight into the resilience of the seeds in which we are entrusted. The assimilation of these things keeps us from declaring a premature time of death of dreams entrusted to those with the capacity to create worlds with their words.

Jesus, the master communicator, used an illustration to establish a critical truth when He said, *"Most assuredly, I say to you, unless a grain of wheat falls into the ground and dies, it remains alone; but if it dies, it produces much grain. He who loves his life will lose it, and he who hates his life in this world will keep it for eternal life"* (John 12:24-25, NKJV).

Jesus' use of words was eloquent yet abrasive; comforting yet somehow simultaneously confrontational. How can someone so loving be so sharp? Maybe love is not what we perceive it to be, and therein lies the problem.

He came to model an invisible reality yet to be revealed. In doing so He kicked against the social norms and religious rhetoric. He destroyed preexisting ideologies that prevented a release of the genuine love that flows from Heaven. In this upside-down Kingdom in which Jesus is King, love and death are synonymous.

> *For God so loved the world that He gave His only begotten Son, that whoever believes in Him should not perish but have everlasting life. For God did not send His Son into the world to condemn the world, but that the world through Him might be saved (John 3:16-17, NKJV).*

THE SILENCE OF DEATH

As far as the Trinity is concerned, has it ever occurred to you that love and sacrifice are one and the same, not at odds with each other, not different things altogether? Instead there is a symbiotic connection that makes them inseparable. By its very nature a seed is a sacrifice. It begins as something you hold tangibly in your hands. You can see it, feel it, and hold on to it as long as you choose. But there comes a time when you release the seed to bury it in the ground, and now it is outside your control. You no longer see it, nor can you monitor its progress; it is outside your control, utterly helpless to protect during that season in which it was planted.

Besides watering the ground, we are reduced to waiting for the seed to germinate in the process of time for harvest. It sounds like a sacrifice to me; it feels like death more often than not. In that time of darkness, your mind is flooded with questions. Will He resurrect what you relinquished? Is He faithful? Are you faithful? In the waiting comes the revealing. Eventually time speaks and tells you all things and often contributes an accurate assessment of the internal components of our heart.

There is no death like a death to self, and there is no heartache like hope deferred. The question remains, who heals the hearts that have grown sick in the waiting? After Jesus had preached the infamous message that minimized the masses, He looked to His disciples and asked, *"Will you leave also?"* Peter's response was classic, *"Where can we go? You have the words of life."* It is possible that Jesus' thoughts reverted to the prophetic words of Simeon about a sword that will pierce the heart of Mary and die a thousand deaths (Luke 2:35). After all, He didn't come to bring peace but a sword.

> *"Do not think that I came to bring peace on earth. I did not come to bring peace but a sword. And he who does not take his cross and follow after Me is not worthy of Me. He who finds his life will lose it, and he who loses his life for My sake will find it"* (Matthew 10:34, 38-39, NKJV).

THE SUFFERING PROPHETS

As far as prophetic words are concerned, these seeds are deeply connected to the soul of a prophet, frequently birthed in hardship through much travail and groaning. They are far more than mere words or empty phrases. As it was with Jesus who endured afflictions and reproach, so it is with the prophets.

These prophetic seeds are the felt heart of the Father released through suffering in the lives of the prophets. The seeds carry the DNA of transformation glory, but those who never labored with the Lord through a dark night of the soul, holding on to the words of life and risking their own life, will never know the deep connection to this process. The cost of these precious seeds is directly connected to the difficulty in which they were attained. Too often the hearers have no interest or context for the price prophets paid to throw the seed before them. Unfortunately, their regard and resolve to steward these precious gifts are often grossly out of balance.

While the prophet's obedience is not contingent upon the audience's receptivity, the process never changes. As a result, the prophet's soul often takes a beating in a manner of which the average believer is unaware. Regardless, obedience is the lifestyle of all prophets. After all, it was Jesus who came to His own but they did not know Him.

It is one thing for someone to disagree with an opinion or disregard a differing perspective; it is something entirely different to experience the fellowship of His sufferings as people disagree and disregard the word of the Lord. There is a grief that cannot rival the heart of the prophet, and the heart of the Father and the prophet beat as one, break as one, and contend for love at a high cost to themselves.

In his book, *Prophetic Ministry*, T. Austin Sparks refers to the rejection of the prophet's words: "They could not hear the voices of the prophets because the prophets were talking about a suffering Messiah, and there was something inside the people which had closed the door; so, they were predisposed against anything like that, and so they could not hear." Sparks comes to a concluding thought with these words, "If you are going into greater fulness of knowledge—I mean spiritual knowledge of the Lord—and therefore greater fulness of usefulness to Him, you must take it as settled that this principle of the cross is going to be applied more and more deeply as you go on. We have seen the terrible tragedy of people who knew the message of the cross in fulness and who are after many years has been a positive contradiction of that very message —marked by self-assertiveness, self-importance, impatience, irritability so that other people have been unable to live with them."

PROPHETIC TIME IS NOT INSTANTANEOUS

Time is on the side of those who walk in patience and tolerance, those who find their hope in the Lord. Character is developed over seasons, involving years of faithful service to God as we perpetually lay our mind, will, and emotions on the altar and in faith, believing that He who began a good work in you can see it through to completion. It isn't about our words after all; it's about His words. They cause the grain to grow, produce seed for the farmer and bread for the hungry, and cannot return void but always accomplish the purpose for which it was sent (Isaiah 55:10, 11).

Similarly, it is not about our words or reputations. As we grieve and groan over what we see, it mustn't be about our reputation, track record, or public image. The moment we slip into this trap of creating a reputation is when we fall into a pit of significant error. We are humble couriers for Christ, not the imperious object; we do not stand before people on our own accord. As we grow in grace, we learn to leverage the ache of our heart with a beautifully broken display of compassion rather than a passionate fit of rage. Being aware that we constantly have the opportunity to manifest one of these two drastically different realities can serve as a guardrail to keep us on the straight and narrow.

There is no shortcut, bypass, or expediting of the process of time. It must be experienced in all of its intricacies and complications. It is essential to sit at times, gazing in the face of painful and even excruciating things during those seasons. The key is learning how to stop and intentionally praise God with much thanksgiving in seasons that seem too good to be true as you jump from mountaintop to mountaintop. Caught in the vortex of excruciating pain, you learn to hate it, love it, embrace it, and then brace for it. You don't need a guru because life is your most prominent teacher.

Through it all, you will learn the faithfulness of your God, the fickle nature of your heart, and the incredible healing power to survive. Traumatic experiences of loss can leave lasting effects on those who experience them. Our most extraordinary story for the world is one of radical wholeness and joyful expectation from those who have experienced the goodness and faithfulness of a God who remains the same yesterday, today, and forever!

So the LORD *used to speak to Moses face to face, just as a man speaks to his friend. When Moses returned to the camp, his servant Joshua, the son of Nun, a young man, would not depart from the tent* (Exodus 33:11, NASB). Like the true prophets, they are friends of God, demonstrating their loving friendship through attentive awareness and loving obedience as God's trusted representatives in this world, not out of obligation but intimacy. In the place of intimacy, slow is a good thing, like it was with Moses; the friendship was not swift but gradual. So take a deep breath, remove the sense of unholy urgency from your processing system, and savor each moment of the journey.

SEEDTIME, THE WORK, AND HARVEST

Harvest is not for the faint of heart. It is not only when we taste and see that the Lord is good but also requires the most work. Early mornings, late nights, and hard days are necessary to gather in the harvest you spent so much time waiting on. It is much like a family that makes radical alterations in preparation for the arrival of a new baby, but the real work begins once the child arrives.

Harvest results from the effective placement of a seed, the necessary process of time, and the ability to discern the times and seasons.

In Paul's metaphor, we are farmers who scatter spiritual seeds across the field of life, some good and some not so good. The rains come, the sun rises, and these seeds will bear fruit at harvesttime. The harvest is determined by the kind of seed used and the different segments of time to process. So the nature of the seed dictates the quality of the fruit, and the timeline dictates how long it takes to reach maturation.

The harvest requires workers, and as Jesus said, they are few, but we need eyes to see the fields that are white unto harvest. Harvest is the season where the most challenging work is done. It consists of early mornings, late nights, and strenuous labor, and it is the hour when fruitfulness is proven! It would be such a shame to see all that has gone into this process come crashing down simply because someone grew weary in doing good. The worst enemy of passionate motivation is time. Humans often have a great beginning and a despondent finishing of the work. So don't lose heart, don't give up, and don't miss the opportunity to partner with God for something bigger than your life. Harvest is where we "taste and see that He is good." The phrase *taste and see* means "try and experience." The psalmist urged people to discover God's goodness derived from personal trial and experience.

Fruitfulness requires knowledge of the full spectrum of all God planned for us concerning seed, worker, time, and the harvest. One is not less than the other; all are necessary for cycles of fruitfulness produced in the lives of the prophets. The cycles of prophetic life consist of these varying facets over time, leading to the ultimate harvest. Our ability to identify the ways of God is essential, so you do not resist His process, which dictates your success and stewardship of prophetic ministry. Eventually, as you walk with the Lord, sowing in every season, you begin to reap in every season as well. Consistency is everything. Remember, it is required that stewards be found faithful.

As I conclude this chapter I will leave you with a challenge. I want to encourage you to take a long and thoughtful look in the mirror. Take an honest assessment of areas of your life that are not fruitful. Why is there no fruit? Once identified, ask the Holy Spirit to search your heart and weigh it against His nature. Have you lost heart? Has hope deferred caused your heart to grow sick? Could it be that you have forgotten the very nature of the God in which you claim to represent, having exchanged intimacy for religious activity?

Whatever God highlights, and He will focus on something, then take the opportunity to posture your heart in surrender to His essence and character. Crucify any lie in your mind, will, and emotions that has risen against who He is. Fruitfulness is rooted in God's faithfulness. Honesty, transparency, and authenticity promote deep levels of intimacy that will result in fruitfulness in all areas of your life. It is my prayer that these truths carry with them an anointing to break cycles of barrenness in your life in such a way that glorifies the Father.

9

GENTLE OFFENSE

"At some point you will have to hurt someone's feelings to save their life. When your motives change from 'saving a life' to 'being harsh,' you've exchanged the spirit of prophecy for arrogance and pride."

Offense is a ministry few have the grace to navigate with the heart of the Father. At some point you will have to hurt someone's feelings to save their life. Correction is not pointless but necessary. But when your motives change from "saving a life" to "being harsh," you've exchanged the spirit of prophecy for arrogance and pride. Gentleness carries varying definitions depending on your disposition. In other words, it is relative to specific situations. Prophetic ministry involves correction and potentially leads to rebuke when necessary. *Open rebuke is better than love carefully concealed* (Proverbs 27:5, NKJV).

Correction requires an acknowledgment of error and repentance and the transformation that follows. Healthy rebuke stems from a relationship that extends beyond correction alone. Accompanied with a consistent presence in the life of the individual, it empowers effective discipline. Your commitment to move in the gentle offense will ensure longevity in ministry and relationships throughout your life.

Have you ever been rebuked? If so, it is awful! There is nothing pleasant about it. It is a public recognition of personal failure, deficiency, or being blindly imperceptive of the issue. Your ability to respond in humility rather than pride dictates your progress moving forward. While there are many ways to move forward, a guaranteed way to stay stuck in your current situation is pride. *Pride goes before destruction, And a haughty spirit before a fall* (Proverbs 16:18 , NKJV).

LEARNING TO LIVE WITH BIBLICAL REBUKE

I have heard it said that the degree of an offense necessitating correction is directly connected to the amount of pride in your life. While personally navigating through penetrating conviction, intense discernment, and a bend towards justice has seldom been rivaled, deep conviction, passion, and zeal will not always accompany a right spirit. Frequently they are at odds with the character of Christ, the process of reconciliation, and the ultimate goal of redemption. It does not mean that you see incorrectly, hear wrongly, or that your discernment on a significant issue is mistaken.   In God's Kingdom, the end does not justify the means. God values the journey and process as much as the ultimate destination. The goal never changes of letting endurance have its perfect result so that you may be perfect and complete, lacking in nothing (James 1:4). Life cannot be proven until it is tested, and be assured, for you will be tried and hopefully proven faithful in the process.

You can't be trusted in the arena of rebuke and correction in the lives of others until you have first endured it personally and successfully arrived at the other side. Otherwise the degree of severity you might administer would be so intense it may break them rather than restore them to the heart of the Father. The ultimate goal of correction is always to create a greater connection with them!

If your thoughts shift to punishment, time served, or simply learning your lesson, it ceases to be redemptive. It is not merely about getting by and surviving the correction but overcoming the issue. That mindset mirrors the old covenant much more than the glorious new covenant in which we exist. The new covenant expression of prophetic ministry is always driven towards reconciliation. Yes, sin must be addressed. And yes, correction is legal. But these things are simply a means to an end. The moment we shift from the focal point of connection to correction as the primary goal, we have slipped into significant error. The sin-focused paradigms have proven to be ineffective in my life and ministry. But a righteousness-centric perspective tends to liberate those walking in deception, minimizing the collateral damage and sin cycles where people get stuck.

The predominant purpose of the new covenant prophet is to reveal Christ. When the dawn of Christ appeared, the shadows disappeared. The solution for sin is revealed in Christ. He suffered in and on His physical body, and for the punishment of sin He was nailed to the cross of Calvary in our place. Rebuke should always stem from a heart to see the Lamb receive the reward for His suffering.

Personally experiencing correction and rebuke gives you the grace needed to help dispense to others. Otherwise we run the risk of removing humanity and compassion from the correction equation. It is common for young apprentices to tattoo themselves before they are released to tattoo others in the tattoo industry. It gives them a deeper experiential understanding of the implications of their application. Much like a tattoo, the application is everything. If administered correctly, it will mark the individual for the rest of their life in a beautiful way that tells a story. The goal is that the deep impressions from experience do not cause an infection that adversely affects the flesh, resulting in an indistinguishable marking. Rebuke can be beautiful or unsightly depending upon how you choose to cope with the internal contents of the heart.

HEALING CORRECTION IN THE CIRCLE OF COMMUNITY

I have often wondered what it would look like if prophetic individuals learned the importance of the relational dynamics necessary for healthy cycles of correction, reproof, and discipline. Everything related to the Kingdom is relational. If it lacks relationship, it won't carry the weight needed to stand the test of time. I once heard Damon Thompson say, "I discipline my children more than anyone else in this world ever will. But I also love them more than anyone else, hug them more than anyone else, and kiss them more than anyone else. As a father, I reserve that right."

It marked me to this day when I realized that discipline is a byproduct of relationships. You should not desire to speak into the lives of those you refuse to love and lay down your life for them. You might say, "Justin, that seems like an unrealistic standard." But I would argue the testimony of Jesus, which is the spirit of prophecy. So as Jesus laid down His life for others, this gave Him the clout to flip tables, rebuke the establishment, expose their motives, and forcefully address people throughout His life.

Rebuke is an invitation to death—death to pride, death to entitlement, and an end to your public image. It also includes expressions of the intense light of the brightness of the glory of God, a light that also exposes, reveals, and uncovers. Not solely for the sake of revealing your indiscretions but also for the sake of removing things that are robbing you of your full potential in God. Pride blinds us to those things in us we have improperly discerned.

Jesus is a picture of God's grace and mercy towards us in that while we were yet sinners Christ died for us. We were dead in our trespasses and sins, but the heart of the

Father towards us was revealed through the face of the Son. Redemption does not simply cover up and ignore sin, but it exposes and reveals to remove, restore, and fully redeem what was lost. It essentially says "this" has to go so more can come. It is why there is an abundance of emphasis in 1 Corinthians 13 on the centrality of love for those functioning with the spiritual gifts.

GRACE-FILLED MINISTRY OF OFFENSE

Due to the old nature, pride is directly connected to our emotions in a manner that few other things can compare to. The ministry of offense by way of rebuke is designed to deal publicly with something privately destroying an individual. It is possible that unfounded rebuke can highlight and expose negative character traits submerged under years of deep woundedness, sin cycles, and brokenness that have not seen the light in a long time.

Love most definitely covers a multitude of sins, but first they must be acknowledged and repented before genuine restoration can happen. Standing at the precipice is the potential for rejection, anger, and relational disconnect, which is typical. This does not equal failure or that you missed it, but they are merely par for the course in the ministry of offense.

Feelings in their proper place are gifts from the Lord, but they can become an unseen force driving them to destruction when disconnected.

Often people inadvertently develop a spiritual worldview closer to a series of trauma responses rather than the leading of the Holy Spirit. This grace-filled ministry of offense exposes lies people are incapable of seeing in their current state. They may curse you now but thank you later. This may take months or even years, but if they belong to the Lord, they'll eventually come around.

One of the tactics in interactions that proves volatile is taking the opportunity to become personally offended, ending with an unholy response towards you. When I use the language of ministry of offense, I refer to a Holy Spirit initiated, proactive attack on the issue of sin for a brother or sister in Christ. Being offended is never an appropriate response for a believer. Thoughts like, *Who do you think you are?* or, *How dare you say that?* are indicative of internal offense toward others by resisting accountability and humility. Remember that once the sin is revealed, acknowledged, and repented of, restoration can come quickly. Apart from it, you can swiftly become deceived and desensitized to the Holy Spirit while walking down a path to destruction.

There are those who undoubtedly in the course of their life will find themselves navigating the complex dynamics of this ministry of offense . In every case, we must resist the innate human urge to exalt our ego, fight discomfort, and hide parts of our life from the Lord and others. I have often said the only sins Jesus cannot deal with are the ones you refuse to give Him. The problem is that people often hold tightly to the false assumption that we only have to deal with sin at our discretion, but nothing is further from the truth.

God established the church for community, family, accountability, and ultimately transformation. Not only for cities and nations but also for you to be transformed into His image from grace to grace and glory to glory. The antithesis of community is isolation and separation, which feeds the lie that no one has access or opportunity to speak to the parts we refuse to acknowledge.

THE HEART OF A YOUNG PROPHET

My heart is that wherever you happen to find yourself in life's journey, take the appropriate time to acknowledge the foresight of God during the uncomfortable seasons that feel more like a loss than a gain. I desire that you can navigate life's mountains and valleys so you can worship in the valley and weep on the mountain.

May the Lord give you the grace to experience the full spectrum of your emotions in a way that points to Jesus and glorifies your heavenly Father by the power of the Holy Spirit. I prophesy over you the grace for your soul will submit to the Father's heart, unleashing a deluge of healthy, holy, and emotional responses to the leading of the Spirit, changing the trajectory of your life. May the Lord grant you the grace to be quiet and learn, the ability to speak up and into the lives of those in your sphere, and the consistency to stand the test of time.

I bless you to receive and release this ministry of offense in such a way that directs you to the glorious work of Christ in you, the hope of glory. I prophesy a deep love that is flowing from the heart of the Father as you navigate through your discernment and discretion, as you bubble up from the innermost parts of your being. I declare a word of grace over you, empowering you to receive abrasive but persuasive words from leaders so you can lean into the pain of sanctification. I release the testimony of my life and journey in the prophetic that you will receive an increased authority to see restoration released during this season of rebuke. This pain is not unto death, but it is for revealing the Gospel of the glory in you!

10

LOVE THEM TO DEATH

*"Some people hate truth and in turn will hate you...
Love truth; love them."*

What is love? It is a provoking question echoed throughout human existence from the very beginning. From our music to movies and deeply rooted in the fabric of our culture is the narrative of love, the silver lining that runs through humanity. Love is a universally understood concept that is still fluid enough to be a topic that can bring great division. Living in the human community is a personal history that contains moments of joy, instants of disappointment, flashes of tender acceptance, heartrending rejection, tender healing, and painful trauma. The relational circle of love ebbs and flows from connected to disconnected, presence to absence. For some it stings more than it soothes, and for others it has the power to pull them into a profound version of themselves. As a follower of Jesus, the lens through which we view love will in many ways determine our successes, failures, and the uncomfortable space in between.

WHAT IS TRUTH?

There stood Jesus, the Truth, judged by the religious leaders whose every action was bathed in lies. Once Jesus was in the presence of Pilate, the questions began. "What is truth?" asked Pontius Pilate, one of the most significant questions recorded in the New Testament. Regardless of the inference or rhetorical nature of the question, I imagine the weighty words of Jesus' response echoed in his mind long after their exchange in Pilate's court. Many fantasize about having the opportunity for a face-to-face conversation with Jesus. Many subconsciously entertain that idea but earning an audience with the God-man might require intentional acts of religious zeal or a life filled with near sinless perfection. But instead we see the just and the justifier on trial, the Son of God standing before an inferior minister of human justice.

Can you imagine the depth of thought in both men's reflections? What a picture! In so many instances we find ourselves crying out for justice, from the news cycle to the Internet to protests and marches in the streets of any given city. Envision if this trial in ancient Jerusalem took place in our time. If so, Christians would have liberated Jesus by force, inadvertently derailing the redemption of humanity through their best efforts.

After the conversation with the religious leaders' accusations against Jesus, Pilate returned to the Praetorium and called for Jesus to be brought before him. Now begins a sequence of questions asked by Pilate leading up to the final question; Pilate has the questions, and Jesus has the word.

The short but potent dialogue starts with Pilate asking this question, "Are You the King of the Jews?"

In a seeming attempt to stir the pot, Jesus responds with a prickly question, "Are you speaking for yourself about this, or did others tell you this concerning Me?"

Frustrated and a bit angry, Pilate doesn't want to engage this man but must ask the question, saying, "What have You done?"

In direct response to Pilate's question, Jesus declares, "My kingdom is not of this world. If My kingdom were of this world, My servants would fight, so that I should not be delivered to the Jews; but now My kingdom is not from here."

A bit puzzled and maybe intrigued with Jesus' response, Pilate delivers the next provoking question, "Are You a king then?"

The whole dialogue advances one to believe that Jesus brought Pilate to this defining moment when He said, "You say rightly that I am a king. For this cause, I was born, and for this cause, I have come into the world that I should bear witness to the truth. Everyone who is of the truth hears My voice."

The conversation ends with this question, **"What is truth?"** And when he had said this, he went out again to the Jews and said to them, "I find no fault in Him at all."

Much like love, the definition of truth in a believer's life conveys radical implications in every area of their life.

We live in a time zone in human history where truth became relative and flexible with no absolutes in a culture adrift. Truth is so fluid that it seems like the entire planet was thrust into an identity crisis.

TRUTH IN A PERSON

This issue is not psychological, philosophical, or even moral; it is a relational issue! The truth is not a fluid ideological or philosophical concept; it is a real person whose name is Jesus.

Jesus said to him, "I am the way, the truth, and the life. No one comes to the Father except through Me (John 14:6, NKJV, emphasis added). Jesus did not merely teach the truth; He *is* truth, the personification of truth, and the revelation of truth.

> *Sanctify them in the truth; Your word is truth. Just as You sent Me into the world, I also have sent them into the world. And for their sakes I sanctify Myself, so that they themselves also may be sanctified in truth* (John 17:17-19, NASB).

In verse 17, the Greek is translated "sanctified in the truth," and in verse 19, it is translated as "sanctified in truth." The theologians make a distinction between sanctified in the truth and sanctified in truth. Jesus prays His Father would sanctify them in the truth, which is Christ. Christ was set apart for God's purposes, and we are now set apart to be consecrated by the truth and to be bathed in truth.

And the __Word became flesh and dwelt among us,__ and __we beheld__ His glory, the glory as of the only begotten of the Father, full of grace and __truth.__ (John 1:14, NKJV, emphasis added).

"Worship God! For the testimony of Jesus is the spirit of prophecy" (Revelation 19:10b, NKJV). The Word of God became flesh and lived among us. Jesus is the literal Word of God in the flesh. We throw these words around thoughtlessly, like truth, glory, and love, but they are effectively employed with specific meanings within the framework of Scripture . They are not fluid or flexile as one might think and possess enough weight to radically alter the course of your life when applied correctly.

What is Jesus' testimony? It is the testimony of the Divine One wrapping Himself in human flesh while experiencing the full spectrum of human existence. He was tempted and tested, undergoing it all without sin. He was falsely accused, falsely condemned, publicly humiliated, and was crucified by those He came to redeem. Taking on Himself the weight of punishment for humanity's sin, He ultimately rose from the ashes of death and the grave with keys in hand! But that's not all. He then ascended on high, giving gifts to His brothers and sisters as He made His way to the right hand of the Father to continue His intercession for you and me.

Who is he who condemns? It is Christ who died, and furthermore is also risen, who is even at the right hand of God, who also makes intercession for us. Who shall *separate us from the love of Christ? Shall tribulation, or distress, or persecution, or famine, or nakedness, or peril, or sword? As it is written: "For Your sake we are killed all day long; We are accounted as sheep for the slaughter." Yet in all these things we are more than conquerors **through Him who loved us** (Romans 8:34-37, NKJV, emphasis added).*

Who will condemn us? For the ever-living Christ intercedes for us as an advocate on our behalf. Who will separate us from Christ's love for us? For He made us triumphant through His passionate love.

There is a powerful lesson to be learned by contemplating the submitted life of Jesus. There is this intriguing verse in Luke 2:52, *And Jesus increased in wisdom and stature, and in favor with God and men* (NKJV). Wow! Many read the Bible without pausing to understand it. Favor with men, I get. Favor with God, well, that makes one pause. It is hard to wrap your mind around the fact that Jesus was able to grow in favor with God. How is this even possible? The writer in Hebrews gives us clues that will help us perceive its reality.

LEARNING OBEDIENCE

*So also **Christ did not glorify Himself** to become High Priest, but it was He who said to Him: "You are My Son, Today I have begotten You." As He also says in another place: "You are a priest forever According to the order of Melchizedek"; who, in the days of His flesh, when He had offered up prayers and supplications,* *with vehement cries and tears to Him who was able to save Him from death, and was heard because of His godly fear, **though He was a Son, yet He learned obedience by the things which He suffered**. And having been perfected, He became the author of eternal salvation to all who obey Him (Hebrews 5:5-9, NKJV, emphasis added).*

Two crucial things must be addressed in these verses. First, Jesus had to learn obedience. Second, by truth He realized that learning obedience could only happen in the context of suffering. Most have never entertained the idea that obedience was anything less than natural or second nature for Jesus throughout His life. If the Gospels are true, and they are, then Jesus set aside His rights as God to fully embrace His humanity to reconcile us back to the Father. In other words, everything He modeled in His earthly ministry was as a man fully submitted to the power of the Holy Spirit.

Removing the option of victimhood or powerlessness was for all who would be swept into the Kingdom moving forward. It is a weighty idea to entertain when considering that Jesus' free will to submit in obedience to the Father was equally as integral to the process of our salvation as the miracles, signs, and wonders. I've heard it said that simple obedience changes history.

What if Jesus woke up one morning and said, "Today I don't feel like submitting." The consequences would be catastrophic! What if the same power that raised Him from the dead dwells in you and me? If you cannot imagine Jesus operating in disobedience, why do you allow yourself that indulgence? It raises a profound question: how many casualties have there been as a result of our selfish ambition and an unwillingness to yield?

Suffering brings a measure of relative clarity like pain, tolerance, endurance, and commitment, which all vary by cause, conviction, and covenant. For Jesus, His suffering was comparable to the mandate and purpose of His life. I have often heard it said that the measure of opposition you face in your life is an indicator of the breakthrough you carry .

Can you even imagine the undocumented demonic opposition that came against Jesus in His lifetime? I have had my fair share of demonic assignments go against me, like slander, accusation, and excessive witchcraft. At no point in time have I ever thought, *This is way worse than what Jesus must have gone through.* But if we understand the assignment on the life of Jesus that was ultimately passed on to us, we can better embrace our cross and follow after Him.

FELLOWSHIP OF HIS SUFFERING

But what things were gain to me, these I have counted loss for Christ. Yet indeed I also count all things loss for the excellence of the knowledge of Christ Jesus my Lord, for whom I have suffered the loss of all things, and count them as rubbish, that I may gain Christ and be found in Him, not having my own righteousness, which is from the law, but that which is through faith in Christ, the righteousness which is from God by faith; that I may know Him and the power of His resurrection, and the fellowship of His sufferings, being conformed to His death, if, by any means, I may attain to the resurrection from the dead (Philippians 3:7-11, NKJV, emphasis added).

There are two perspectives to consider related to the fellowship of His suffering. People understand why Jesus suffered but do not understand why we suffer. The question is not why the righteous suffer but why some do not! As Jesus suffered, so shall we. In the ring of suffering, Christ and us, we enjoy Christ's presence with us in the fellowship of suffering.

The other perspective also brings pain, and it would not be preposterous to imply that rejection by those He came to redeem, including Judas and Peter, was not without much anguish and heartbreak. *He came to His own, and His own did not receive Him* (John 1:11, NKJV).

Have you ever been rejected by those assigned to you by the Lord? In my opinion there is nothing more excruciating within the scope of ministry than that of rejection for simply being obedient to the call of God on your life. Have you ever been in a season where you were completely content, fruitful, and totally enjoying your life when suddenly the Lord asked you to uproot everything to do something in which you had no interest?

Let's say you manage to stir up the perfect mixture of faith, enthusiasm, and obedience to leave the people you love and the environment you thrive in and then go to people you do not even understand. That alone is a feat worthy of some level of acknowledgment.

Now that you have arrived and begun surveying the

territory, assessing the task at hand, and evaluating the people you were sent to, you realize some profoundly unfortunate realities. Not only are the circumstances unfortunate, but the people don't even like you. The startling actuality of the implications of your decision comes rushing in like a flood, nearly knocking you off of your feet. You begin calculating what you sacrificed for what you perceived you would gain. If you have not experienced this yet, you have not been walking with the Lord for very long. Once you have experienced this predicament, the only question remaining is, what will you do from here?

The fellowship of His sufferings is far more profound and overwhelming than the mere physical pain experienced through the events of the crucifixion. It is not that the physical elements of the process of crucifixion are not significant or weighty. However, it would be grossly inaccurate to reduce the human condition down to merely physical experiences of pain. The soul of man (mind, will, and emotions) and the spirit are equally as intricate, multifaceted, and significant as far as the process of redemption is concerned. During the life of Jesus, the hardships He experienced are as meaningful as those culminating in His death. What we physically suffer without has some finality, but the emotional pain within lingers while torturing the mind.

THE TEST OF LOVE

I titled this chapter, "Love Them to Death," for a reason. Love is not tested until sacrifice has been made. Many would label love as a mutually beneficial relationship with a shared compromise for the greater good, when in reality love lays down its life for the sake of another. It is the testimony of Jesus in the spirit of prophecy .

*This is My commandment, that you **love one another as I have loved you.** Greater love has no one than this, than to lay down one's life for his friends. You are My friends if you do whatever I command you* (John 15:12-14, NKJV, emphasis added).

We often find ourselves mindlessly quoting Scripture, attempting to label a moment in our lives we have trouble reconciling. Many Christians treat the Bible like a medicine cabinet, which they only open when they feel sad, depressed, or need some breakthrough. Few will take their daily vitamin dose and only return when they experience a deficiency. But we overcome by walking in the essence of Christ, whose DNA runs through our veins.

And they overcame him by the blood of the Lamb and by the word of their testimony, and they did not love their lives to the death (Revelation 12:11, NKJV). The overcoming is not based upon who we are but on what Christ has done. Our victory is built upon the victory on a cross. Entirely analogous is the relation in Revelation 3:21 that uses a similar language, *The one who overcomes, I will grant to him to sit with Me on My throne, as I also overcame and sat with My Father on His throne* (NASB). By reversing the order the priority is fixed on Christ, the foundation for all we do. The victory of the Lamb is a shared victory, adhering to the truth in their suffering and not loving their lives, being willing to sacrifice their lives to the death for others.

The Spirit of prophecy would be our testimony, but only if we are willing to follow in the footsteps of Jesus by sacrificially laying down our lives for the sake of others. Our words, which contain the power of life and death, must attest to the power at work inside of us, choosing to love at all costs. Those words, blood *and* the testimony, take us back to Hebrews 9:14, which speaks of the necessity and the power of the blood of Christ, *how much more shall the blood of Christ, who through the eternal Spirit offered Himself without spot to God, cleanse your conscience from dead works to serve the living God?* (NKJV). And verse 22 establishes a biblical reality, *and without the shedding of blood, there is no forgiveness* (NASB). Some things require bloodshed. Not all things, but definitely some things.

Jesus told His disciples in John 20:23 upon their commissioning, *"If you forgive the sins of any, they are forgiven them; if you retain the sins of any, they are retained"* (NKJV). Little did they know the tremendous cost associated with this particular commissioning. The disciples had just received the Holy Spirit through the risen Christ, "in the flesh," breathing on them the breath of God! Jesus said, "As the Father sent me, I also send you." I wonder if they heard the words of Jesus, feeling His breath on their skin as they entered into their reward by way of martyrdom. We fail to realize these profound implications, reminding us that the crucifixion, death, and resurrection were a present reality for them as they experienced this moment where the very breath of heaven kissed their skin.

The weighty word of their testimony and exploits lived during their earthly ministry did not exempt them from spilling their blood to advance the Gospel of the Kingdom. What a testimony!

The apostle Paul makes this statement in 1 Corinthians 4:20, *For the kingdom of God is not in word but in power* (NKJV). And Romans 8:11 says, *But if the Spirit of Him who raised Jesus from the dead dwells in you, He who raised Christ from the dead will also give life to your mortal bodies through His Spirit who dwells in you* (NKJV).

The Spirit who raised Jesus from the dead is the same Spirit who lives in you. In verses 12 and 13, Paul says that we are debtors, not to the flesh, to live after the flesh, but if by the Spirit you continuously put to death the activities of the body, you will live. We are not debtors to the flesh but to the Spirit.

For I consider that the sufferings of this present time are not worthy to be compared with the glory which shall be revealed in us. For the earnest expectation of the creation eagerly waits for the revealing of the sons of God (Romans 8:18-19, NKJV).

THERE IS POWER IN THE BLOOD

In John 15:13, Jesus said that *greater love has no one than this, than to lay down one's life for his friends* (NKJV). But in Romans 5:8 we are reminded that God shows His love for us in that while we were still sinners, Christ died for us.

There is something undeniable about the profound demonstration of power released through an individual that lays down their life for another undeserved. It is as if heaven and earth stop to take notice of this divine demonstration of supernatural love. It demonstrates that the prophets are not exempt from life and death with weighty and eternal significance. After all, we are mere ministers of the new covenant, full of glory, with a banner of reconciliation.

I am reminded of the old Gospel song I used to hear growing up in my Baptist church:

There is power, power, wonder-working power
In the blood of the Lamb;
There is power, power, wonder-working power
In the precious blood of the Lamb.

If the testimony of Jesus is the spirit of prophecy, then the testimony of Jesus rings true in the lives of the ministers of the new covenant . As Tertullian mentioned with these classic words, "The blood of the martyrs is the seed of the church."

I would remind you that this glorious new covenant in which we are a part of is established through bloodshed—not by force, but rather through radical submission unto death at the expense of one for the benefit of all. This testimony of Jesus is an invitation to put our *mission* in *submission* to the Great *Commission*.

LOVE THEM TO DEATH

So when the opportunity materializes to love someone in opposition to every conviction and core value you possess, love them to death! Love is not proven until it is tested, for sacrifice is not sacrifice until something is surrendered, and mercy is manifested by the magnitude of the offense against you.

In closing, I leave you with a portion of Scripture and some powerful quotes that communicate more than I could adequately articulate.

And so we know and rely on the love God has for us. God is love. Whoever lives in love lives in God, and God in them. This is how love is made complete among us so that we will have confidence on the day of judgment: In this world we are like Jesus. There is no fear in love. But perfect love drives out fear, because fear has to do with punishment. The one who fears is not made perfect in love. We love because he first loved us. Whoever claims to love God yet hates a brother or sister is a liar. For whoever does not love their brother and sister, whom they have seen, cannot love God, whom they have not seen. And he has given us this command: Anyone who loves God must also love their brother and sister (1 John 4:16-21, NIV).

"You know you're in love when you can't fall asleep because reality is finally better than your dreams" (Dr. Seuss).

"The opposite of love is not hate; it's indifference. The opposite of art is not ugliness; it's indifference. The opposite of faith is not heresy; it's indifference. And the opposite of life is not death, and it's indifference" (Elie Wiesel).

"Just when you think it can't get any worse, it can. And just when you think it can't get any better, it can" (Nicholas Sparks, At First Sight).

"Tis better to have loved and lost Than never to have loved at all" (Alfred Lord Tennyson, In Memoriam).

"Never love anyone who treats you like you're ordinary" (Oscar Wilde).

"Where there is love, there is life" (Mahatma Gandhi).

11

PERFECTION IS NOT REQUIRED

"Learn to appreciate progression apart from perfection. Acknowledge growth and encourage those around you. Contend for encouragement!"

For those with a gift of spiritual sight, moments of transcendent reality create a sense of delight, but with the gift comes an immense weight of handling present unseen experiences and probable realities that might manifest unexpectedly. In all honesty, those spiritual realities are subject to change as the interpretation of this vision is articulated by those recipients trying to process the information from a completely diverse cultural position, spiritual perspective, and emotional stability.

In many ways prophets are the chain links connecting the anchor of God's words to the ship, which is the person who needs a fixed and stable point of reference. They do not dictate, nor do they edit the word of the

Lord, but rather, they weigh its emerging expression by the Spirit of God. It can prove to be a grueling task for those entrusted with our glimpses of future versions of and the surrounding world.

Prophets are purists, constantly contending for an invisible goal yet seen in its fullness by their peers, like an architect with a detailed set of blueprints in their mind's eye, unavailable to the skilled laborers partnering with them to see this dream become a reality. As the adage goes, "A picture is worth a thousand words." Many times prophets are guilty of holding the picture so close to their chest that no one else has the opportunity to use their God-given ability to discern and see elements they may have missed. In a failed attempt to solve this prophetic conundrum, they fumble in a feeble attempt to describe the intricate details of their heavenly visitation with an ill-equipped arsenal of words. I have witnessed firsthand the detrimental effects of prophets with limited vocabulary and tunnel vision have had on various cultures and human expressions.

LIMITED VOCABULARY

I see limited vocabulary as an inability to express the heart of God connected to the unwillingness to expose themselves to diverse perspectives, cultural expressions, and Scriptural perspectives without predetermining emphasis and context but adhering to denominational party lines. Your predisposed views and core values linger in a combination of family, cultural, and traumatic experiences having hard-wired you to engage the world around you in specific ways that limit pain, negative experiences, and failure. The prophetic is no different, so soul management and managing your mind, will, and emotions are of utmost importance. Ignorance or negligence of the internal components of your heart can have massive repercussions for the prophets.

*A good man out of the good treasure of his heart brings forth **good**; and an evil man out of the evil treasure of his heart brings forth **evil**. For out of the abundance of the heart his mouth speaks (Luke 6:45, NKJV, emphasis added).*

Bypassing the unpleasant, ugly, and even traumatic experiences connected to people's engagement with the prophetic would be great. It is not only possible but it is also a reality so practical we constantly overlook it by prematurely advancing into things we inaccurately deem more critical. But it is remedied by taking the appropriate time to build adequate foundations for the words, utterances, and declarations with the capacity to create new worlds. We are impatient beings often disinterested in the disciplines of establishing strongholds of character, consistency, and longevity.

Limited vocabulary—small-minded, fenced in with vague language for communication. Vocabulary involves your intellectual speech relative to education and your life experiences, which are determined by what you see and the perceived outcomes developed in the formative years of your life as a result of your environment.

If you reverse engineer your limited vocabulary, you

will find that everything is deeply connected to your humanity. For the prophet, humanity is the vehicle through which God has sovereignly chosen to clothe with the Spirit and deliver His rhema word. To ignore, alter, or bypass this reality will quench the work of the Holy Spirit and diminish the power of the cross.

To realize this reality opens the door to plumb the depths of the human experience and find the redemptive power of the cross. But if you ignore, suppress, or devalue your human elements while handling the words of God, this leads to sterilizing God's word and making them impotent and ineffectual. Perfection is not required or even expected. Passion, pursuit, and purity are necessary to eliminate the pit of introspection that limits His realities to our experiences.

TUNNEL VISION

Tunnel vision occurs for those with a drastically narrow line of sight that affects peripheral vision, fading to black. The habitual tendency or the conscious decision to only focus one's energy or exclusive attention on one particular thing or aspect without regard for anything or anyone prevents a more spacious perspective. This is a common occurrence in the natural, but for prophets the results of prolonged tunnel vision can be catastrophic. You must understand that emphasizing unity and uniformity are not the same thing. Within the circle of unity, diversity is allowed without disruptions, but within uniformity, positions and perspectives are fixed.

There is one body and one Spirit, just as you were called in one hope of your calling; one Lord, one faith, one baptism; one God and Father of all, who is above all, and through all, and in you all. But to each one of us grace was given according to the measure of Christ's gift (Ephesians 4:4-7, NKJV).

As believers in the Lord Jesus Christ, grafted into the family of God, we are not awarded the opportunity to ignore or disregard the life and work of our siblings. The gifts, call, and anointing may be radically diverse, but the source remains singular. I find it profoundly significant that Jesus, knowing this reality, prayed the way as He did in John 17.

"I do not pray for these alone, but also for those who will believe in Me through their word; that they all may be one, as You, Father, are in Me, and I in You; that they also may be one in Us, that the world may believe that You sent Me. And the glory which You gave Me I have given them, that they may be one just as We are one: I in them, and You in Me; that they may be made perfect in one, and that the world may know that You have sent Me and have loved them as You have loved Me" (John 17:20-23, NKJV).

JESUS' DIVERSITY IN MINISTRY

Undoubtedly on His Father's assignment to redeem humanity to the glory of God, Jesus made wine for a wedding, found time to stop for the woman caught in adultery, liberated the demonized man in the Gadarenes, and spent time with children. Such diversity is profound and deeply significant for the prophet to realize. Jesus could have been so laser-focused on the cross that He could have walked past the blind man, ignored the invalid at Solomon's Porch, and overlooked Zacchaeus and the dinner that changed history. Depending on your heart's condition, the burden of the gift of sight will determine what you choose to focus on and disregard. It does not mean the mandate is insignificant or negotiable; it does mean the way we choose to engage it determines whether or not we see some glory or greater glory.

Jesus, knowing the diverse expressions of the Spirit, was about to be poured out without measure, praying for oneness, not unity. Unity carries with it the idea of separate things coming together for the sake of a singular purpose. Oneness implies there is no separation but of similar origin.

Why is this important? It is foundational, not only for prophets but every believer. Overemphasis on self-will without fail lead you into cycles of fruitlessness as your focus shifts from Christ and Kingdom riches to you and your role, function, and purpose in the greater scheme of things. Jesus was the Son of God as one with the Father, on course for the cross, and yet with His eyes fixed on the cross, He paused, stopping to laugh, cry, eat, sleep, pray, and intersect with the lives of those He came to redeem.

BEWARE OF BURROWED VISION

Tunnel vision entraps you. You focus so intently on the object in front of you that you ignore your journey with the Holy Spirit, where you never know where the Spirit will lead you. If Jesus walked through life in perfect cadence with the Father's heartbeat and still hit the target of the cross, then this is our option.

No destiny is so significant that it will supersede the process, including the times and seasons the Father holds in His hands. No mandate is so urgent that the King cannot interrupt it to model both His lordship as well as His great wisdom.

While not necessarily indicative of sin but unchecked, it could result in unnecessary collateral damage. I tend to be so laser-focused on the task at hand that I have the propensity to negate or significantly neglect other elements entrusted to my stewardship. Focus is a good thing; uncontrolled obsessions can be detrimental for you and those around you. A healthy prophet is a balanced prophet.

We must develop the ability to hold our reality and spiritual truth in tension. With the ability to harness the winds of change and propel us into the future, the sail of sight must be connected to the anchor of discernment, giving us the ability to know when to hold on and when to fold. If at any point you are going too fast to stop for the nudging of the Holy Spirit, then you shifted from the *leading* of the Holy Spirit to a personal *driving* force, which can be influenced by the unholy *pull* of partially revealed prophetic perspectives. But if you take a moment to slow down, recalibrate your focus, and take a look around, you will find the tunnel was an illusion.

Perfection is undoubtedly not required because God

is consistently in the center of the process, a road more traveled with failure, mistakes, disappointments, and constant adjustments. God desires to meet you in your inadequacies to display His strength while you trust Him to take those imperfections and make something uniquely and distinctly holy unto Himself.

Surrendering to the seasonal sting of the process is a foundational element, often unspoken, in the lives of seasoned seers and prophets. If you examined a broad spectrum of prophets throughout history, you might be surprised to find that the most consistent similarity is one of failure. No one likes to fail when a loss is so painful. But these are the things that develop character and endurance in those of us who aim at the prize of our high calling in Christ. The choice to embrace failure as a friend and loss as a lesson will prove extremely valuable in your journey with the Lord.

THE NECESSITY OF CONNECTION

"You were never intended to operate alone! Belief in anything contrary will encourage arrogance, pride, and everything detrimental to you and your ministry. Rejection gives you no right for removal!"

Human connection is a concept seldom grasped by mystics and prophets. For those prophetically shaped in isolation, the pull to the private places is strong, sometimes resulting in them turning their backs in the broader community, like Jeremiah, Elijah, John the Baptist, and other prophets who chose or were forced to spend too much of their lives in the desert, that place where it's just the prophets and the voice of God. Much of their time was spent in meditation, intercession, and solitude.

The prophet's call is one of obscurity, opposition, and varying levels of hardship that most cannot comprehend. For many, they live with their head in the heavens with their feet barely touching the earth's terrain. It is as if they are the silver cord between humanity and divinity. The spiritual connection can be so strong and intuitive that the natural human connections become problematic.

However problematic, it does not exclude the prophets from engaging in the relational dynamics of the Gospel as they walk this life out in pursuit of the Kingdom. Jesus, who was fully God, surrendered all entitlements for the sake of fully embracing His incarnation and engaging the world in which He lived. In doing so, humanity was introduced to the opportunity to reconcile with the Father and connect with His Son.

In managing the word of God, we must constantly engage with the reality that our *lives* and *words* are the cumulative expressions of God towards others. It was true for biblical prophets, and it will continue to be true for modern prophets. In a postmodern world where isolation continues unless connectivity escalates through community and communion, the foundational elements are necessary for successful Christian living.

BALANCING PROPHETIC MINISTRY WITH HUMAN CONNECTION

Though Jesus often chose seclusion in the desert or a mountain for prayer and conversation with His Father, He did not live a life of independence, isolation, or disconnection. When there is a prophetic word, message, or declaration, there will also be an audience. God does not need to prophesy to Himself, nor does He need to amend His perspective. Intimacy is necessary, and ministry unto the Lord is nonnegotiable for prophets and priests but can be done without eliminating human connection.

Jesus lived His life up close and personal with the disciples, simultaneously fulfilling His Father's will. The crowds of people could sense that Jesus was moved with compassion for the sheep without a shepherd. Amazed by every move Jesus made, the people watched in amazement as He flipped tables. Then after a series of healings and instructing the people, He pulled away to be alone with the Father in the wee hours of the morning. If Jesus lived His life in isolation, there would be no Gospel stories detailing miracles, teachings, mentoring the disciples, and monumental moments that altered the course of human history. The diversity of human connection and personal solitude also applies to us as well.

The Lord intends that our lives be lived fully on display before heaven and earth with Christ's fragrance on us drifting up into the Father's nostrils. The supernatural intersection between divinity and humanity is the tightrope in which the prophets walk as the world around them watches with intrigue. Navigating the tension of what was, what is, and what is yet to come is a feat not for the faint of heart. However challenging it may be, the difficulty does not deter the elect from their mandate. It is why the clarity of the mission is irreversible in the life of the prophet.

CORRECTLY PERCEIVING WHAT YOU RECEIVED

I will stand my watch and set myself on the rampart,
and watch to see what He will say to me, and what I

will answer when I am corrected. Then the LORD answered me and said: **"Write the vision and make it
plain on tablets, that he may run who reads it. For
the vision is yet for an appointed time; But at the end
it will speak, and it will not lie.** *Though it tarries,
wait for it; Because it will surely come, It will not tar-
ry.* *"Behold the proud, His soul is not upright in him;
But the just shall live by his faith" (Habakkuk 2:1-4,
NKJV, emphasis added).*

The context to these verses is the prophet's pleas and
arguments with God, and now he waits to see how God
will respond. When God speaks, there is no rebuke but
a word of prophetic direction. In a concise staccato style
of communication, God declares what the prophet must
do, but we don't know the vision. Absent from the context
of the sight in which prophets operate, we can become
overstimulated so we cannot disseminate the information coming in our direction. If we lose sight of the *vision*,
it will adversely affect our *perception*.

Your roots will determine your reach, and if your
reach exceeds your depth, destruction is near. Time is
your teacher, comparison your enemy, and the process a
platform in which you will stand as a messenger of the
Lord. What you see will often exceed what you know, and
what you know will determine what to do with what you
see and hear. What you know is relative to your experience, education, and maturation at its highest levels of
expressions, understanding, and competence. You will
not be trusted to lead where you have not first learned in
the school of the prophets. The lessons you learn today

determine the landscape of tomorrow. Your wilderness experience transforms into the Promised Land at the speed of obedience.

What you carry is precious and holy unto the Lord. Sight is your gift, knowledge your responsibility, and reconciliation your mandate. Wisdom manifests in your life as sight and insight merge in a beautiful display of submission to the Great Commission. Yield today, wield tomorrow. As far as the Kingdom is concerned, victory is found in your consistency.

ISOLATION AND SEPARATION

The remedy to pride, ego, and all subtle measures of vanity hiding beneath the surface of your heart is unveiled in community, which is the remedy of destruction that comes with isolation. There is safety in a multitude of counselors and strength in numbers. While there may be moments of retraction like a Sabbath rest and intentional solitude for contemplation and prayer, this is not intended to be constant.

Accountability is best described as giving an account for your ability. While you will most definitely answer to God for every word spoken, you also need to stand ready to provide a confident answer to the leaders, communities, and those with influence you aim to communicate prophetic messages.

Jesus often pulled away from the crowd, His disciples, and even His family to spend time with the Father. There is a difference between separation and isolation.

Separation with affirmative purpose—the Hebrew

and Greek meaning of separation is not isolation because in biblical separation one separates from one thing or people to join another, as illustrated in 1 Chronicles 12 , *Men of the tribe of Gad, who lived on the other side of Jordan; these separated themselves from the rest of their tribe, from their families and dwellings, and from the government of Saul, and came over to David, and joined him.*

And then in 2 Corinthians 6:17, it says to *"Come out from among them and be separate, says the LORD"* (NKJV). The story of Paul and Onesimus is an excellent illustration of separation for a purpose. Onesimus, a former slave, stole things from his master, Philemon, then fled to Rome, where he met Paul in prison and was saved. In the letter to Philemon, Paul says that *perhaps this is why he was separated from you for a while, so that you might have him back for good* (Philemon 1:15, BSB).

Isolation with adverse purpose—one of the Hebrew words for isolate occurs in Leviticus, and the biblical word refers to quarantining the unclean. But Proverbs 18:1 makes it clear that isolation opposes community because of pride and offenses, *A man who isolates himself seeks his own desire; He rages against all wise judgment* (NKJV). And in standard Hebrew the word for isolate is, which means to segregate and be apart.

Strangely enough, following a great victory on Mount Carmel, Elijah escapes Jezebel, runs away, and isolates himself in the wilderness, depressed, angry, and ready to die. Pity parties are often ill-attended, sulking with me, myself, and I in an unhealthy cycle of negativity and self-talk that is toxic behavior. The great prophet of God has sunk into a horrible display of pitiful depression, which gets you nowhere. *"It is enough! Now, LORD, take my life, for I am no better than my fathers!"* (1 Kings 19:4, NKJV).

Jeremiah is another sulking, sensitive prophet in a difficult place. When God said that *even* if Moses and Samuel stood before Me, My mind *would* not *be* favorable toward these people; he was hurt and felt a great burden. The intensity of God's rhetoric in chapter 15 left Jeremiah in a state of depression when he cries out, "Woe is me," and "I wish I were never born." And God hasn't done anything yet. All God has done is share His secrets with the prophet. But Jeremiah wants to isolate himself from those who think he has done them wrong, and his words are oppressive. The thing that grips you is how God graciously manages the sulking prophet and brings him back to his calling. Prophets are not meant to live alone but in community.

HEALING AND HONOR IN THE COMMUNITY

Edification, exhortation, and consolation for others are the endgame of the prophecy, and yet prophets are often the hardest on themselves, giving little grace and no mercy while navigating life's challenges. We often speak of prophets receiving no honor in their hometown while rarely addressing the lack of recognition we ascribe to ourselves internally.

It is a needless epidemic in the prophetic because it is remedied through community. I once heard Dr. Mark Chironna say, "You cannot know yourself by yourself." So often prophets highlight the negative statements while neglecting to acknowledge the encouragement that often comes as our peers celebrate our parts that we fail to perceive. We allow fear to blockade our hearts from those who could potentially hurt us while failing to realize their potential to heal us the way God intended.

More often than not, fear is a self-fulfilling prophecy. The only problem with this form of prophecy is that it need not be uttered to be effective. One must hold it to be true internally for it to manifest externally. Our ability, vulnerability, and willingness to stare headlong into the face of frustration, irritation, and disappointment concerning community, connectivity, and accountability will dictate the scope and scale of our prophetic ministry in life.

If we cannot apply the ministry of reconciliation and restoration to our earthly relationships in a way that believes the best, contends for wholeness, and suffers long, then our ministry will only carry a little weight. It creates quite a conundrum for the prophets because they are the minority of the squeaky wheels, whistleblowers, and individuals who cannot remain silent amid injustice. But I'm not telling you anything you haven't learned through the unpleasant seasons through which you have navigated. But hope is the answer to the puzzle because we have an anchor to the soul that goes behind the veil where the reality is Christ in us, the hope of glory. If we place our trust in anything less, we will be found lacking the supernatural expression of the Spirit.

INCEPTION AND CONCEPTION

Inception and *conception* are the gates of passage from heaven to earth. While the two processes most definitely have their fair share of differences, they are not that dissimilar. Inception is the starting point of an institution or activity. Conception is the biological conceiving of human life at its earliest state. Words are seeds, seeds are words, and the timing, placement, and life are often left in the sower's hands.

T.S. Elliot, poet, publisher, and playwright, beautifully articulated this process in his poem, "The Hollow Men":

Between the idea
And the reality
Between the motion
And the act
Falls the Shadow
For Thine is the Kingdom

Between the conception
And the creation
Between the emotion
And the response
Falls the Shadow

The shadow is the birth canal of the Kingdom. The apostle Paul gave language to this deep place of shadows where the Spirit hovers over the dark and troubled waters. The hidden wisdom of God wrapped in a mystery can only be revealed by the Spirit. Inception is the realm of the secret place where epiphany enters this earth realm. *Merriam-Webster* defines an *epiphany* as, "a moment in which you suddenly *see* or *understand* something in a new or very clear way." Kim Clement, one of the most significant prophetic voices of the last one hundred years, made the statement, "The oracles of God speak because they have seen. Before there is a word, there is a thought, generated by what one has seen."

Through the Holy Spirit, God opened a door of revelation so we might understand the depths of God and speak the language of God.

> *However, we speak wisdom among those who are mature, yet not the wisdom of this age, nor of the rulers of this age, who are coming to nothing. <u>But we speak the wisdom of God in a **mystery**, the **hidden wisdom which God ordained before the ages**</u> for our glory, which none of the rulers of this age knew; for had they known, they would not have crucified the Lord of glory. But as it is written: "Eye has not seen, nor ear heard, nor have entered into the heart of man The things which God has prepared for those who love Him." But God has revealed them to us through His Spirit. For <u>the Spirit searches **all things, yes, the deep things** of God</u>. For what man knows the things of a man except the spirit of the man which is in him? Even so no one knows the things of God except the Spirit of God. Now we have received, not the spirit of the world, but the Spirit who is from God, that we might know*

*the things that have been freely given to us by God. These things we also speak, <u>not in words which man's wisdom teaches but which the Holy Spirit teaches, comparing **spiritual things** with **spiritual**</u>. But the natural man does not receive the things of the Spirit of God, for they are foolishness to him; nor can he know them, because they are spiritually discerned" (1 Corinthians 2:6-14, NKJV, emphasis added)*

The New American Standard says combining spiritual thoughts with spiritual words.

Though Jesus' departure caused the disciples to become concerned and a bit insecure about not having His presence, Jesus reminded them how better it was for Him to go so the Father could send the Holy Spirit, who would reveal all things to us. Jesus encouraged them, saying we would go on to do the same works and even greater because He was going to the Father on our behalf. Jesus did not only carry the words of the Father, but He *was* the Word of the Father. The perpetual process of Jesus moving from the secret and quiet place into the public arena only to repeat it over and over again was an invitation to unforced rhythms of grace, known as the heartbeat of the Father.

Your decision to bring these words, seeds, thoughts, and divine epiphanies to full term and birth them into the world will determine the effectiveness of your earthly ministry. The art of taking what is conceived in secret through divine communion and representing it in the mature form to the world around us is not for the faint of heart.

It comes with an abundance of challenges and obstacles along the way. It is not convenient, easy, or even enjoyable on occasion. However, it is the mandate in which the prophet is tasked. Unfortunate as it may be, it requires presence and intentionality in the community and all things social.

The necessity of connection cannot be overstated as you pursue your God-given call in your life. Prophets are messengers, mediators, and in ways moderators between God and man. A life of isolation will prove to be fruitless and frivolous overall. God has not designed us to be independent but interdependent throughout our human experience. It was the eternal Godhead who took a long look at Adam in the garden and said, "It is not good that man be alone." It does not solely refer to marriage and the act of procreation, but rather the deep-seated need hardwired into our spirit, soul, and body that longs for connection.

I urge you, contend for connection, fight for family, and aspire towards accountability. It is my prayer that as you pursue the profound call of God on your life, you are met with abundant supply from heaven. I hope you have a profound awareness of your inability to accomplish your tasks apart from divine intervention and an unrivaled dependency upon the Holy Spirit daily.

May the Lord bless you, keep you, and cause His face to shine upon you in every season.

MEET THE AUTHOR

Justin Allen is an internationally recognized speaker, author, and advisor to leaders in every arena. He has become a friend, encourager, and counselor to individuals in all walks of life. Dr. Randy Clark personally mentored Justin as he interned with him traveling the nations on the frontlines of revival where He received powerful impartation. He is a graduate of Global Awakening School of Supernatural Ministry, a former Associate Evangelist for the Ministries of Global Awakening, and a globally recognized prophetic teacher, trainer, and equipper.

Justin has ministered the kingdom preaching, prophesying, counseling, training, and equipping in over 10 nations, over 30 states, more than 50 cities, and upwards of 60 conferences globally with miracles, signs, wonders, healings and deliverance following all before age 35. Justin is a husband, father, and lover of the Godhead.

He ministers with a heavy prophetic edge through teaching, training, and equipping the body of Christ to hear the voice of God and release the kingdom on earth as it is in heaven. Justin operates in a unique boldness that releases the gift of faith in individuals who seem to feel like a victim of circumstance. There is a great grace on his life to administer revelatory prophetic vision plainly and in a fashion the believer can run with. Justin's heart is to see the kingdom released in all nations and people restored through pure and powerful prophetic ministry.

ACKNOWLEDGMENTS

I would first like to thank the incomparable Don Milam for his patience, consistency, humility, and willingness to work with me as I attempted to unearth the deepest elements of my heart and soul. Without his counsel, encouragement, and persistence, this book would have remained an open document on my computer that would never have seen the light of day. I am forever grateful for your friendship and mentorship. Thank you for your commitment to the Lord and servant heart towards the prophetic movement!

To my spiritual father, Dr. Randy Clark, words cannot adequately express your impact on my life in every arena. The risk you chose to take on me by investing so much of your time, effort, and resources will forever confound and humble me. You exposed me to the frontlines of global revival and renewal, ruining me for anything less than the glory of God in every area of my life. My time with you in the nations is eternally etched into my consciousness and has changed me for the better in every way possible. I love you, Randy. Thank you for modeling humility and hunger in a way that glorifies Jesus!

To Dr. Mark Chironna, your intentionality, compassion, and tender wisdom in the darkest season of my life sustained me when I couldn't see out of the pit. You saved my life and sanity and allowed me to see hope in the valley of Achor. Thank you for modeling prophetic integrity, excellence in academia, and a resolve that is second to none. I will forever hear your voice in my head in a tone that only someone who had already navigated the path could confidently state, *It won't always be this way, Justin.* I love you, Mark. Thank you for your steadfast commitment to authenticity and rightly dividing the Word of Truth!

To my spiritual mother, Dr. Kim Maas, your wisdom is unrivaled. Your consistent presence in my life has been a wellspring of life, hope, and encouragement. I am forever grateful for your prayer, counsel, and investment in my life. I thank God for allowing our paths to cross, merge, and intersect over the years. Your consistent encouragement has spurred me to believe the best about myself when my emotions refused to engage with my destiny. I love you, Kim. Thank you for being in the trenches with me as well as on the mountaintops!

To my beautiful bride, Amanda. God knew what He was doing when He joined us together in His sovereignty over thirteen years ago. We've celebrated on the summits, crawled through the valleys, and wrestled through the ups and downs. We've birthed things, buried things, built things, destroyed things, and somehow, after all these years, we are stronger, wiser, and gentler than ever before. I am eternally grateful for your patience, compassion, and commitment over the years. Walking alongside someone like me is not an easy task and comes with its fair share of warfare, weeping, and work. I love you and look forward to many more years of love, laughter, and advancing the Kingdom through our family. Thank you for not giving up on us and honoring the covenant we made so long ago!

To my blue-eyed beauties, Aaliyah, Hope, and Cana. Being your father is the highest honor and privilege I have ever been able to steward. I pray that the words I've written in my dark night of the soul will serve as a light to your path in times of my absence. I leave you my diaries of love, loss, and the faithfulness of the Lord throughout my life. My testimony is both your foundation and inheritance as you press forward into all that God has for you. I am so grateful for your love, encouragement, and the immeasurable joy that comes from my time with each one of you. Wherever life takes you, remember the still, small voice of the Lord is as close as the air you breathe. Daddy loves you, God loves you, and the prophetic promises over your life *will* stand the test of time!

ENDNOTES

CHAPTER ONE

Accessed August 19, 2021, https://www.spurgeon.org/re-source-library/blog-entries/8-spurgeon-quotes-on-the-trinity/

CHAPTER FOUR

T. Austin Sparks, *Prophetic Ministry,* accessed April 3, 2020, https://www.austin-sparks.net/english/books/001004.html.

Ibid.

CHAPTER FIVE

Accessed November 2, 2021, https://www.goodreads.com/quotes/455720-if-we-desire-our-faith-to-be-strength-ened-we-should.

Bill Johnson, *Strengthen Yourself in the Lord,* accessed October 2, 2021, https://www.goodreads.com/work/

quotes/751227-strengthen-yourself-in-the-lord-how-to-release-the-hidden-power-of-god.

Ibid.

CHAPTER EIGHT

T. Austin Sparks, *Prophetic Ministry* (Shippensburg, PA: Destiny Image Publishers, 2005), 53, 54.

CHAPTER TEN

Accessed October 27, 2021, https://biblehub.com/commentaries/john/17-17.htm.

Accessed October 28, 2021, https://www.goodreads.com/quotes/7901-you-know-you-re-in-love-when-you-can-t-fall-asleep.

Accepting the Nobel Peace Prize, in *New York Times,* 11 December 1986, accessed October 28, 2021, https://www.oxfordreference.com/view/10.1093/acref/9780191826719.001.0001/q-oro-ed4-00011516.

Accessed October 28, 2021, https://quotecatalog.com/quote/nicholas-sparks-just-when-you-t-N700Y37.

Accessed October 28, 2021, https://interestingliterature.com/2021/01/better-loved-lost-than-never-loved-origin-meaning/.

Accessed October 28, 2021, https://minimalistquotes.com/oscar-wilde-quote-3114/.

Accessed October 28, 2021, https://www.pinterest.com/pin/519321400753763088/.

CHAPTER TWELVE

Accessed November 2, 2021, https://www.wordhippo.com/what-is/the/hebrew-word-for-4ee64af0b2223831d-706d10af4775feb24fca81c.html.

Kim Clement, *Call Me Crazy but I'm Hearing God* (Shippensburg, PA: Destiny Image Publishers, 2007), 141.